The Magic of Engagement: Education's First Step

Leah R. Kyaio, M.Ed.

DEDICATION

My perspective is that no one really reads the dedications. I'd love it if you prove me wrong. Email me at
leahURwrong@with-respect.com
Let me know you actually read this; In your email, include at least one reference in this dedication and see what kind of gift might show up in your email inbox.

This book is dedicated to the Ancestors and to the Seventh Generation.

ACKNOWLEDGMENTS

The journey for this book has been a lesson for me in breaking through my own challenges. Without the following people, it probably wouldn't have happened and certainly wouldn't have happened this well, right now.

Kathleen Gage. As the first "professional" who ever believed in me (and said so), you offered encouragement, wisdom, and support that were the first step in the birth of this book. Thank you.

Judy Sorrells. Your patience in the artwork of this endeavor is truly appreciated. You are an artist of many mediums; paper and heart. Thank you.

Patty Krisher. Your expertise in understanding my voice and supporting me in making sense has been worth a thousand words. Your skill as an editor with integrity is worth even more. Thank you.

Ebie Andrew. Thank you for loving me into and through this. You are my first and perpetual cheer leader. I can't imagine life without you. I love you.

Anna, Patch, Sean. You have taught me more than any degree I hold, any experience across my life. It is because of you, for you, and for the generations after you that I hope this book takes on a life of its own. Thank you!

CONTENTS

INTRODUCTION.

Engagement is the *magic*[1] of true education. It's about getting students to the table as willing participants in learning. It's about reinforcing content and making learning fun and relevant. It's the gateway to everything "education."

From preschooler to adult, without engagement NOTHING happens. How can it?

35% of all U.S. students report disliking school. 61% find school boring. The result? 49.6% of the adults in the United States read at an 8th grade reading level or below. When you don't like school and find it boring, you don't learn… BECAUSE YOU'RE NOT ENGAGED!

That's what you can change with the strategies and activities I've outlined in this book.

This book is all about the what, the why, and the how of the *magic* of engagement. It's designed to be informative and cutting edge as a text, a resource, and a spring board.

The first part of this book is divided into chapters that outline the strategies and concepts of engagement. It's the what and the why of connecting with your students and keeping them connected. It's not about **entertaining** them. It's about **engaging** them.

Each chapter is followed by questions for your consideration, individually or in groups, that are intended to help you integrate the information and take in at a deep level of core understanding; to get it in your bones! These questions are intended to prompt reflection and can be answered as a solo practitioner or in pairs, small groups, or professional learning communities. I want to give you every opportunity to look inside yourself as you move through this book.

---

[1] When you read this word, hear tinkling bells of wonder and happiness!

The second part of the book provides the how. It begins with the nuts and bolts of 20 activities, how to set them up, what you need to make them happen and how you can vary them based on your audience, group size, and even cultures. Each activity is set up with the description (including materials and set up time), the correlating strategy/ies with explanation, and some possible variations to the activity. My intention is that by understanding what each activity does and why, you can begin to create and implement your own new and tailored engagement activities.

Throughout Part 1 & 2, there are references to the "Magic Resources." This is near the end of the book, a page that allows you to connect to a special web page where you can download many of the resources needed for the activities as well as videos, research links, and other resource links.

It's not the expectation or requirement that you use every activity in the book. It is necessary, however, that you understand engagement deep in your bones. That's how you improve as a teacher, by getting the *magic* inside of you. Most importantly, that's how students (from birth to adult) succeed – they feel the *magic* of engagement that you present!

We are all simultaneously teachers and learners, no matter our personal or professional path. True education enrolls us at the cradle and graduates us at the grave. That is the point here. Whether you are a classroom teacher, a para-professional, administrator, company CEO, professional development trainer, or consultant, the concept of engagement is relevant to what you do. I hope you will find the content and activities to be useful beyond the concept of formalized education. Think about the applications of everything discussed here to life and how we live our journeys.

So let's get started!

THE MAGIC OF ENGAGEMENT

Part 1.

THE WHY & HOW
OF ENGAGEMENT

Ch. 1. THE BEGINNING.

Embarking on this journey as an Education Hack (Self-defined as a person creating solutions to problems in education that support the teaching and learning process for every learner) began in so many ways within the story of my own education.

I was an inner city thug, born into a family where drugs and guns were the family business. I was brought up through the ranks, a rough life at best (yes, that's a different story). I learned that I didn't really want to "inherit" the business. When I started looking around, it became clear that the only way out was through education.

Did I mention I was an INNER CITY thug?

The urban education system was *not* a system that *granted* learning. No, you had to *fight* for anything you wanted. On top of that, there was no family value in education. My father had an 8th grade education and my mother a 6th grade.

I had to **want** an education. I had to ignore the expectations for "those kids." I had to figure out what classes I needed for college and then fight to get them. I had to answer questions and turn in homework even when it wasn't really expected. Sometimes I even had to trick teachers into helping me figure things out.

In the process I found two allies; a school counsellor and an English teacher. Finding information was difficult. There was no internet. There was a library with a paper card catalogue system. But you had to KNOW what you were looking for. Without those two allies, I never would have been able to find what I needed.

With their help, although I was the youngest of 8 grandchildren, I was the first one to graduate from high school and the only one who went to college. I now have a bachelor's degree in psychology, a master's degree in education/special ed and an almost-PhD in educational leadership and administration.

What about all my classmates who didn't have those allies, who didn't know they had an opportunity they had to fight for, who didn't know there could be more out there? Many of them didn't live through their 20's. Indeed, of those 8 grandchildren only half of us are still around.

The high school I went to warehoused kids. They didn't learn who we were, what we wanted, needed, dreamed about or cared about. They certainly didn't provide us with an education. As a result, few of us performed well. Many dropped out and moved into life on the streets doing what they needed to do to survive. A lot of them wouldn't do that.

Indeed, I was often chastised by teachers for asking questions. I was identified as a trouble maker (not that I was by any means angelic!) and spent a lot of time in the principal's office. I challenged and demanded my learning. Some teachers rose to the challenge, reveling in my desire to learn, something so foreign in their classroom walls.

But those two educators *saw* me. They acknowledged, not only my existence, but my goals. They were the first people in my life who ever told me I was smart, believed in my ability to get out of the trap I was in, helped me find what I needed, and got me on the right road to college. They encouraged me to look for my angle, to work the system to my advantage.

I had a musical background (that's a different story, too). They encouraged me to take up a new instrument, to use that as my angle. So I did. By the time I graduated from high school (3rd in a class of 400+ students) I was 9th in the state on tuba, 15th in the state on trombone and landed a full scholarship to a highly recognized music college on trumpet.

The story certainly doesn't end there and was by no means easy, but I did it anyway. Without the beginning support from those two educators, my feet would have travelled down the familiar path of inner city thugs.

Yet, no one should have to work that hard to get what is their inherent right in this country. Free, appropriate, public education (FAPE) is a right granted to every child.

As I worked in education, I saw that my experience was not unique, that education is not something that was easy for kids to get, particularly kids of color, those with a disability or who came from poverty. Appropriate educations are far from the norm; one size fits all is much more typical. True education was not something that most adults know how to provide. One thing was sure; I wanted to change all that.

As a teacher for traditional learners and those with identified special needs, I began to understand deeply what I had known innately as a child – kids learn from people they have relationships with, people who are or become their community. That it is all about ENGAGEMENT.

I practiced and tried things out on my own classrooms, my own kids at home and, ultimately, on the adults that I began to teach, train, and coach.

You know what? It works!! When you engage the learner – from the beginning all the way through the experience – they learn AND THEY LOVE IT!

Welcome to the *magic* of engagement.

That's where it began for me. This is where it continues, so we can all provide for every child, every learner, their right to a quality education.

+++++++

What's your story? Consider why you do what you do – whether teacher, educational aide, administrator, trainer, development specialist, CEO, general learning leader - and how it relates to your experience in education.

Ch. 2. RELATIONSHIP BUILDING

Engagement is all about relationships.

That's it. Period. After all, each of us is willing to do more for those with whom we are connected, more for the communities for whom we are contributing members.

Think about your own educational experience. What are the things that jump out at you? What grabbed you? Encouraged you to work harder, do more, be more? It's unlikely it was some life changing content. More than likely it was a person; it was about a *relationship*.

It's true for our students as well. They need to connect with us in order to be willing to take the risks involved in learning.

As teachers, parents, trainers, facilitators, para-educators, and administrators we are the identified leaders of young children, adolescents, and/or adults. As those leaders; whether in a classroom, a boardroom, the kitchen table or the playground; we are responsible for creating, nurturing, guiding and growing our relationship with each and every student.

Each and every one.

I remember my experience as a young teacher, my first classroom. It was a K-5 special education, self-contained room. I had become a teacher because I love kids. Now here I was, in my own classroom with real students! I was so excited!

Then... I discovered the child... *the* child that I didn't like. No real reason, probably just a personality clash. Regardless, I didn't like her. I was horrified! I love kids, especially these kids, MY kids! How could this happen?

But no, this child... I just didn't like her. I was devastated.

Of course, then I started thinking about it, started realizing that I had to give her exactly the same quality education I gave to the other students in the room. I had to engage in a meaningful relationship with her that was authentic, compelling, and nurturing.

That brought another realization. Within my classroom, every student needed the same quality relationship with me to be able to be safe enough to make mistakes, brave enough to celebrate even the littlest triumph, and happy as a unique individual contributing to the community of our classroom. That was true for my "favorites" and my "challenges." Each. And. Every. One.

That was the beginning of my deepened understanding of what engagement means as a leader. It was my realization that **I must be engaged** to engage. I can't just follow the motions of some activity like a recipe and expect results. If I'm not open and willing to connect, there can be no real connection. If I try to fake it, people know it in about three seconds flat. It has to be authentic.

I have to be engaged.

Relationships just don't work any other way. If I'm not engaged in a conversation, you might as well be talking to the wall. Without my willingness to meet you, we can never get to the restaurant let alone to the table. I have to be engaged first.

What does it look like to be engaged? It's the same stuff as what we do in all our relationships.

Engagement is *active*. That means I'm doing things.

For example, there is *eye contact*. When someone is speaking to me, I look at them. Depending on their culture and their personal preferences, I might make direct eye contact. I always provide the non-verbals when I'm listening to let them know I am attentive and attending to what they say. If they gesture in a direction with the intention for me to look that way (on their paper or near the board) I look where they're pointing. I do my best to not interrupt and to follow the details.

The art of active engagement also includes *questions*, both asking and responding. This is done to check for understanding and clarifying information. As the leader, you ask questions and you ask *for* questions.

Similarly, you are *responsive*. This extends to laughing when a student is appropriately funny (and sometimes not-so-appropriately), catching them being good, and monitoring for their engagement.

Lastly, is *validating* (which is often part of questions and responsiveness). Whether I repeat back what they've said to ensure clear understanding or whisper quiet words to acknowledge something they've done well, I am always looking for ways to validate people, to remind them that I notice and that what they are doing is important and worth mentioning. Validation requires respectful, constructive review that is genuine and includes praise and criticism when appropriate.

I have to open the gate for them to walk through. People WANT to be ENGAGED. Most of what we as leaders need to do is LET them. Kids want to do. They aren't invested in being bored. We have to meet them half way and give them something to do, something to latch onto, a reason to engage.

What about those "Engagement Challengers"?

There are those students and participants who are identified as:

- Unmotivated
- Disenfranchised
- "Prisoners"

The Engagement Challengers.

They are often the ones who sit in the back of the room or in a corner. They might slump down, occupy themselves with something else, sleep, or otherwise work to do their best to ignore you and everything going on around them. They might even be the hecklers or trouble makers. If they are disruptive, they certainly impact the learning environment for everyone.

After a few attempts, most folks write them off, do the best they can to manage that corner of the room and keep moving forward.

For a moment, think about what we've been talking about here....

Engagement is about relationships.

What's at the core of relationships?

Push comes to shove, relationships are built on need. Need is driven by behavior. Behavior has three paradigms that are all true and true all the time:

1. Behavior meets a need. All behavior. It's *all* about getting needs met.
2. As long as the need is met, the behavior won't change. Why should it? If it ain't broke, don't fix it.
3. Behavior doesn't just stop; it has to be replaced.

Now let's apply that to our Engagement Challengers. Their behavior, whether passive or active, has always worked to allow them to remain unconnected, un-engaged. If it hasn't worked all the time, it's worked most of the time. Otherwise, it wouldn't have continued.

But why?

Most of our Engagement Challengers are those who struggle with the learning process. Maybe it's the "sit and git" model they can't work with; perhaps it's that they process slower than material is provided. Perchance the material is way below where they process, or it could be that they've taken in negative messages about who they are as members of a community, as a learner, as someone who might need the information being provided.

The question becomes, what will make YOU different from those who have come before you, who have reinforced the beliefs behind the behaviors?

Theory tells us that awareness leads to belief, leads to action, leads to commitment.

Awareness → Belief → Action → Commitment

This process has been true for all learners, but is particularly noteworthy for our Engagement Challengers. Let's say that our particular Engagement Challenger believes they aren't smart and so use their engagement challenging behaviors to avoid having to be part of the learning experience and thus reinforce, publicly that they can't learn.

How did that happen? At some point, a teacher, instructor, coach, trainer, parent, and/or all of the above focused the learner's *awareness* on some part of what they couldn't do, something that couldn't be performed as it should. The learner took that criticism of the lack of performance as about their ability, about being smart or smart enough. Then every "failure" was internally attributed by the learner to be the result of the same lack of ability, the same lack of smarts. In this way, awareness became *belief*. Then come the behaviors – the engagement challenges – the *action* that allowed the learner to avoid the uncomfortable awareness and potentially be able to use an "I couldn't care less" attitude to save face in the community and, as a consequence, become an outsider to the community. At this point, the cycle is strongly in place and the learner has a *commitment* to the behavior to avoid the awareness of what they now believe to be true about themselves.

Here you come to break down that whole misconstrued process. Are you ready?

Of course you are! You have the *magic* of engagement!

Relationships are based on need. Consider why your students need you. Why should they want to be in this relationship, the one called learning, with YOU?

First and foremost, they have to believe you care about them, that you have their best interest in mind, that learning with you is safe.

You prove those truths in the learning environment you create. You create the learning environment by creating the culture, climate, and community of the classroom, all of which are based on the relationships within, across, and among the participants.

That's what the activities of engagement do. By choosing what you will use, when, and how, you are intentionally influencing the impact of the environment on the participants within that environment. You intentionally influence the relationships and consequently develop and mold the culture and climate. That's how connections happen, how communication is used, how community is built and nurtured, and how conflict is managed.

In so doing, you invite each learner, including the Engagement Challenger, to the table. Those who quietly resist often require one on one interaction to reduce the high stakes they may perceive.

Let's take an Engagement Challenger who tends to do nothing during class. When there is a prompt for the group to respond, there is no response. Perhaps he doesn't take advantage of volunteer opportunities and maybe stares off somewhere else when I'm talking or during small group time. I would want to notice this early on and work toward resolution that doesn't waste precious time. At the same time, I want to be sure that there has been enough time for natural engagement – the idea that everyone else is involved and it's fun and it's working – but he's not come around. I then would approach the student, one on one, privately. It would look something like this:

"Hey, Daniel. What's going on? I see you're kinda spacing off during class. Is everything okay?"

"Yeah. I'm good."

"So, what will it take to get you to be part of things? I want to make sure you are learning and enjoying this class. I have no doubt that your thoughts and how you learn are an important contribution to your classmates and to me."

"I don't know."

"Tell you what. I'm going to pair you up with Adrien. He tends to need a little extra support sometimes staying on task. He's also really smart and might be able to help you out sometime if things are a little hard to follow. Would that be okay?"

"I guess."

Understand that I haven't done this in a vacuum. I've already talked to Adrien who indeed needs some help sometimes staying on task. He also really has a good command of the material and is willing to help Daniel should the need arise. Adrien has agreed to be Daniel's "engagement buddy" so they both stay connected during class time.

I've seen this concept of 'engagement buddies' work more than once in many different ways. It's how I use the community to engage an individual or small group.

Think of it as a set up for success. It can even be set up from the beginning where everyone in the community has an engagement buddy. It serves as a group mechanism to keep each individual engaged and connected. It is one of those tools that, when the momentum you are creating in the learning environment hasn't caught each learner, you can focus the momentum a little more in the direction of specific learners.

There are all kinds of ways to use engagement buddies. They can become Elbow Partners (pg. 94), be part of Rotational Instruction (pg. 89), and ideas of accountability partners and check-in buddies.

Remember Daniel? Because I engaged one on one with him, I have created a clear correlation that I care about him. As part of the mindset, I will follow up with him along the way, checking in and staying active in the relationship between us. This is true for all the learners in the room. As the leader, it is my job to notice that which is out of the ordinary or when poor habits or tendencies become ordinary.

You see, engagement is about relationships. For those Engagement Challengers, it's just necessary to do a little more to make the relationship work. None of your students have to adore you, they just have to engage in a meaningful, respectful, working relationship with you. That's engagement.

It's not about warm fuzzies.

That concept of a meaningful, respectful, working relationship doesn't require warm fuzzies. Some of us naturally interact in warm fuzzy ways – with lots of praise, and intimacy - and that's okay. Some of us don't, and that's okay, too. Warm fuzzies work for some kids and for some it doesn't. Regardless of warm fuzzies, meaningful, respectful, working relationships have five characteristics:

1. Connection – between the leader and the learner and between learners. This is the core of the relationship. It is about the community.
2. Clarity – in expectations and communication, both ways.
3. Predictability – the behaviors between the parties are pretty much always the same. When they aren't, the connection requires a check-in to find out what changed.

4. Openness – this is like honesty but doesn't require the intimacy of honesty. Openness is the ability to say "I made a mistake" or "You made a mistake" without offending. It also provides for the foundations of honesty – thinking about the file folders I used for each student in my high school classes (See Check In/Out in Activities, pg. 63). The file folders created the openness and some of the students extended that to a level of intimate honesty. It wasn't about warm and fuzzy; it was about openness.

5. Safety – who I am in any given moment is safe. It doesn't mean I won't be held accountable, but there is no intention of physical or emotional harm. Safety is paramount to creating an environment where learning can happen.

These five things don't require soft and cuddly warm fuzzies. They require engagement – yours and theirs.

It's about relationships.

That's the core of it all… As the leaders and teachers we have to know how to create these meaningful, respectful, working relationships within a safe learning environment. And it has to be true for ALL learners.

+++++++

Are you engaged? If not, how will you get there? If so, how do/will you stay there?

What are the most important parts of building relationships that you need to focus on this year?

What are your greatest fears related to relationships in the classroom? How do you overcome those fears?

Ch. 3. ENGAGE CONSTANTLY

The thing about engagement is it's not something you do once and are now done doing. It has to happen ALL the time. Remember, you are actually nurturing relationships. Relationships don't just keep going based on the first act of connection. They have to be constantly nurtured, supported, balanced, and activated. The same is true of engagement.

There is always the first impression, of course. This is the first opportunity for opinions to be formed. Often times, first impressions are foundational for the relationship. Makes that first day of class take on a bit of a different perspective.

From the moment they walk through the door until the moment they leave, they need to be engaged.

Focus their attention

There's a lot of information out there, especially in an age where we are competing with constant info overload. Leading educational experiences (i.e. teaching) means you are shining a light on what you want them to be focusing on, what the learning in here is all about.

Being able to focus their attention requires engagement and engagement requires focusing their attention. It's part of the package in the relationship.

The safety of the relationship means there is a level of trust. That means if I as the teacher say, "Look here" the learners know that it is important and safe to look there.

Focus #1: Culture & Climate

That first week of class (or the first 10 minutes of a training) is the "get to know you" time period. You are also building the foundations to your management – rules, guidelines, habits, expectations – and to your classroom culture.

The culture of the classroom (the habits, expectations, etc.) then come together to establish the climate (how it all feels, how it flows, etc.). It all develops right alongside the relationships. This is what I call the "before."

It's like all the work that goes into the set-building for a stage production. Without the perfect set for each scene, the focus at any point during the production will be easy to miss and the experience will be compromised.

Focus #2: Consistency

Once the initial foundations are laid, consistency will be the word you need to make your best friend. Consistency is required to make those foundations truly become habits to nurture the relationships. This is the practice that will span the entire time you are together – whether it's for a short period of time or a full semester or school year. Consistency is how it will become comfortable, predictable, and just how it goes.

Through consistency comes the safety and space for learning.

Engagement activities that are part of consistency are what I call the "in-between" activities. This is the time that fills in the cracks of the learning time, the times when students are not necessarily focused directly on content. Most often these are times of transition, whether between subjects, classes, locations, or tasks.

Not so ironically, it is during these transition times that students often find themselves in trouble. They wander off the road of learning and get engaged in social scuffles or interruptive behaviors. It is crucial, then, that engagement continues through these times by the consistency of habit and expectation and through the activities that guide and encourage the appropriate focus.

Focus #3: Content

The entire purpose of engagement is effective content delivery. It seems logical, then, that engagement must continue into, through, and around content. This is a good time to emphasize the difference between engagement and entertainment. While there is nothing wrong with entertaining learners and it can certainly be part of successful engagement, it is not all of it. If the only engagement utilized is entertainment, when the entertainment is over, so is the engagement.

When I'm teaching, the goal is to provide the information in a way that is interesting, accessible, and encourages higher order thinking. This is, of course, developmentally aligned with the age and ability of the learner.

Higher order thinking is like a pyramid built on remembering, understanding, applying, analyzing and/or evaluating, and creating. It looks like this:

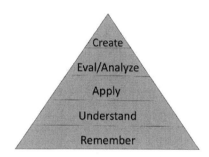

Engagement is the tool we use to move learners from the bottom to the top of the pyramid. When I think about learning in this process, it makes sense to me that I have to provide those I teach with the opportunities to move up the pyramid. Until a learner owns the material enough to be able to apply it, learning hasn't even begun. True education isn't about just being able to remember information on cue or even simply to understand what is provided. True education, the art of making information mean something useful, begins with application. The executive order processes of evaluation, analysis, and creation are where the electricity actually lights the lightbulb.

It is through engagement that I offer these opportunities "during" content delivery.

Relating to Part 2 of the Book

You will see that the activities in the second part of this book are identified as BEFORE (B), DURING (D), and IN-BETWEEN (IB). While I have gone to great lengths to explain my perception of these delineation, please don't get married to those exact concepts. Allow me to explain.

Some of the activities identified as BEFORE could be categorized as IN-BETWEEN, and that would be valid. However, I tried to make them make sense and, as the one writing the book, I got to pick where some things went.

DURING activities are those designed to be implemented with the delivery of content. They could be looked at as instructional design or foundation of delivery.

Since one of the objectives of writing this book is to enable and encourage you to create your own activities, know that you have the same latitude as you create your own activities. Before, in-between, and during can mean whatever you want them to mean. The real point is that engagement is required constantly.

There is little excuse for un-engagement though there may be times of dis-engagement. What's the difference?

Those learners who are un-engaged aren't connected. There's been no reciprocity in the reaching out, reaching into a relationship. As the leader, it's your responsibility to figure out how to engage every student. If what you're doing isn't working (and when you're done with this book you will have lots of choices of what to do) then go find some more things to try. Every human has a need for connection. Learning REQUIRES it. They don't have to like you, they do have to engage in a relationship with you. Make it your mission to find a way to have a relationship with every student. Don't forget: every single one.

Throughout the journey together, there are times when some learners are more engaged than others, times when dis-engagement happens. That disconnection may or may not have anything to do with you, but it is your responsibility to regain the connection as soon as possible.

That's why constant engagement is so critical.

In the best of all possible worlds, I hope to have every learner in any environment with me from the beginning. Sometimes that doesn't happen. Then I have to notice as I move forward, work to engage them directly with me. I might wander in their direction. Make eye contact. Ask them a question directly. I don't want to embarrass them, that's not going to help. I want to invite them, validate that I care to have them, specifically, as part of the learning community. I might quietly ask if there is something they need or, if I notice a distraction, what it might take to regain their attention.

That's the point of Chapter 2 – it's about the relationship.

Building on that, engaging constantly is taking care of that relationship, nurturing it and making sure it is exactly what is needed at any given time.

Engagement is so much more than what we do and when we do it. It's the complexity involved in all professional relationships. It's the ebb and flow, the give and take, the difference between what works and what doesn't.

+++++++

Think about your experience as a learning leader. How often have you known, for sure, that your learners were engaged? Think about what worked and what didn't.

Is there a time in a learning environment that is easiest for you to create engagement (introduction, beginning of an experience, during, in-between)? What is the most difficult time?

What do you do when you don't have all the learners engaged?

Ch. 4. PRIOR KNOWLEDGE

When I get something new to file in my office, I don't have to go back and create a whole new filing system. New material gets filed within the system that exists. If it doesn't fit within that filing system there's a good possibility I will throw it away. Exceptions would be if I understand how it relates to some other part of my filing system which allows me to make a new file folder.

The same is true of new learnings. As a learner, I file what I am learning into my brain's filing system, the one that already exists. That filing system is made up of all my prior learning and experiences, all my prior knowledge. If what I am learning doesn't fit within that filing system there is a strong possibility I will not identify it as important and I will throw it away. If I understand how it fits with something already filed, I can likely create a new "file folder" and store the information appropriately.

Organization is crucial to my ability to integrate, retain, and recall information. Not only is it about storage of information, it's about retrieval. Where information is stored is only half the equation. The other half is being able to find it when it's needed. If I can't find where I put it, then I can't access it later.

As learning leaders, we have to create the connections to prior learning. This can be subtle or blatant depending on the topic. Engagement is about creating that connection. It's not just about the relationship between the learners. Engagement is also about the learner's relationship to the content.

Incidentally, there are people who experience processing and recall delays or disabilities. By understanding and planning for organization and connections from the beginning of content delivery, it is possible to create strategies for those who struggle with processing, retention and recall challenges.

There can be a challenge in any learning environment to ensure that what is being presented connects to all the cultures and experiences represented in the room. It is particularly true in professional development and training that bring a potentially eclectic group of people together for short periods of time. There is no guarantee that everyone has the same life experience or cultural context.

This is why I often create a common learning experience, a new file folder. At the same time, I link that experience to something already familiar to the group. This provides me with a translation point I know exists because I created it. I can call on it and refer back to it throughout our time together.

The best example I use often in trainings, presentations, and learning experiences is what I call the "Ball of Perspective." (If you've EVER experienced me as a learning leader, you've been part of this experience.)

It involves a 6" ball, half one color and the other half a different color. For this example, let's say one half is blue and the other half is red.

I ask for two volunteers who come up front with me, facing each other. I place the ball between them so that the red half faces one and the blue half faces the other. I then ask each of them, "What color is your ball?" They respond by their correlated colors; red or blue.

Next question to the one looking at the red half, "Will they ever convince you your ball is blue?"

They respond, "No."

To the one with the blue half I ask, "Will they ever convince you your ball is red?"

"No."

To them both, "What will it take for you to believe that your ball could be a different color?"

The responses provided (and if not provided, I provide), "The ball would have to move or I would have to move."

"Yes, thank you. You can both sit down."

I now go on to correlate this to the concept that each of us has our own perspective, made up of our life experience and interpretations of that experience, we all see our "ball" as one color or another.

I remind them of what can make up perspective and give concrete examples and information, connecting to what they know and what they think they know. I talk about the fact that the first time we spend the night at someone else's house we discover new ways of doing things – sleeping with a light on (or off), pet routines, etc.

I often tell the story of my own son, who grew up in a house set up for the Deaf, meaning there were lights that flashed for phones ringing and doorbells. The first time he spent the night at a friend's he came home excited, "Mom, their phone RINGS!!!"

I discuss that we all agree and understand that everyone has their own perspective yet are surprised and sometimes outraged when people have perspectives different from our own.

This exercise then provides me with a strong foundation throughout the learning experience to reinforce and reflect on the idea of individual perspective. Questions posed from personal perspective like, "Why don't they just (whatever)" can easily be referred back to the experience in a way that provides depth and meaning to our own perspectives and their impacts on what we think, see, feel, expect, etc.

This is effective as a bridging tool, providing a "new file folder." Because I don't have any way of knowing for certain what any one in that room holds within their perspective, I bridge from what they have as their perspective to what I want them to understand as the concept of perspective. I have created a common experience that correlated to their prior knowledge that I then use to expand and respond throughout the learning experience.

In this way, a word that we all use – perspective – takes on a common meaning and a common experience. It allows me to push the learning forward in ways that I couldn't do if the group lacked a common understanding of that word.

This is what connecting to prior knowledge provides; context. It establishes the parameters of the learning and provides someplace to file the information. That makes it easy to continue learning AND to recall the learning later. It also improves the engagement because all the learners are functioning from the same frame of reference, there are no assumptions.

Connecting to prior knowledge is extremely useful when the content is compounding. Examples include things like math and writing where often the next level of content builds on the previous. By intentionally connecting them with examples that are as concrete as possible, the prior knowledge is reinforced AND the new knowledge is connected to what has already been filed.

Considering this component of engagement as one mechanism to create clarity is also helpful. By making connections between prior and current learning, the learner and the content are also connected. This goes a long way in preventing the feeling of being lost and confused. It also increases the likelihood that if a learner is lost or confused they have enough information to formulate a question.

Prior knowledge is the stepping stone for future learning.

+++++++

How does the content of this book build on your prior knowledge? Why is that important?

Do you have any new insight into how you might support the connection of new material you are teaching to prior knowledge?

Think about or discuss how creating a common experience can support bridging cultural and experiential differences in your learning environment.

Ch. 5. CONNECT TO REAL LIFE

"Why do I have to learn this?"

This is a question that is heard often in the classroom. The wrong answer is, "For the test."

If that's the only correlation to the content that you can provide, don't expect learners to truly learn the material. Oh, they can, and probably will, memorize or otherwise arrange for the specific information to wander around in their brain until the test, where they will regurgitate it to be able to get what they need from the testing experience. However, as our diagram of higher order thinking from Chapter 3 reminds us, this is one of the lowest levels of thinking; remembering.

In order for learners to be able to truly synthesize concepts to be accessible later and contribute to future learning and processing, they have to make their way up the pyramid of higher order thinking. They have to become understood to be applied and applied to be able to be used to evaluate, analyze, and create.

In chapter 4 one mechanism of supporting that synthesis was discussed, that is, connecting to prior knowledge. Connecting to real life adds the nuance of application that prior knowledge may or may not include. It is the idea of linking what is being learned to the thinking and doing of every day. Prior knowledge provides context while connecting to real life provides relevance.

That is not to say that everything taught is relevant to real life and some things aren't simply learned for the test. We all have those things we had to memorize for the test but promptly forgot once the experience was over.

There are also those tricks to memorization that lead to some trivia-type information that is stored forever. Mnemonic devices and rhyming are examples of the tools used to ensure information is virtually etched in the stone of our brain. I still recall the musical staff lines by the F.A.C.E. acronym and recall the grammar rules of rhyming like "i before e except after c."

Music is another similar mechanism and the reason I can sing the lead song to television shows like Gilligan's Island and The Brady Bunch (and, yes, I'm dating myself!). I'm sure the same is true for you.

Such tools are important and very useful in engaging students in the art of remembering details and information that may otherwise be outside of the context and relevance of their recall.

But if what we want is for learners to be able to own information and concepts and be able to build on them and use them to analyze, explore, consider, and formulate opinions, then we have to provide relevance. That's what connecting to real life provides.

In creating the culture and climate of the community of learners I build, I have the opportunity to correlate the skills and strategies that I use to the relationships beyond the learning environment. This is the idea of connecting to real life.

Since respect is a core concept for me and all environments I'm in, I can easily create the connection between the strategies I teach and the things known outside of the current environment.

For example, I define respect for the learning environment I create I use an acronym. I create a more concrete vision of what I mean when I say respect. My acronym (found as a poster in the Magic Resources):

Remember

Empathy

Sincerity

Patience

Compassion

Truthfulness,

allows insight into my expectations. Continued conversation will expand on those words as vocabulary builds and I will correlate those words to specific behaviors I see. In this way I am building the bridge between the world my learners know that is outside of the learning experience to the world I am creating within my walls. That creates the connection to real life. It is a point of reference that allows us to speak a common language.

Thinking about what we teach as it connects to everyday life is easier in some areas of content than others. However, if what we teach is to be relevant and applicable (and why would we teach it if it were not?) we have to make clear those connections for our learners. In providing the connection we make the learning real.

I have found it to be true that many learners have trouble making any leaps or assumptions. I may very well know how teaching about women's suffrage relates to the importance of all eligible voters registering and voting but I do not leave it to assumption. I state it clearly, "The reason we are learning this in our class on civil liberties is to make sure you understand how important it is for all eligible persons to register as voters and exercise their right to vote."

Connecting what is learned to an activity or behavior reinforces the learning. It is likely that when the discussed behavior occurs, there will be a tag back to the learning experience.

Another example I use when defining diversity is to use a common, daily behavior. "The only place diversity is not found is when you're standing alone in the bathroom looking in the mirror. The rest of your life, you are engulfed in diversity."

People often chuckle. Humor is another important connection that also reflects "filing" has happened.

That chuckle indicates the connection has now been made to a common behavior of looking at oneself in the mirror. My intention is the next time the learner looks at themselves in the mirror, they will remember the definition of diversity.

Project learning is one great mechanism to make connections to real life and across content. One example is the second through fifth grade classrooms that designed and built the new playground for their school. With the help of community members, they integrated;

- Math – budgeting, design and construction of equipment and space
- Humanities – designing a fully accessible playground
- Writing & Communication – they created a proposal for the school board and request letters to community members for participation and donation as well as the thank you letters when it was over.
- Computers – research for what was possible and to connect to another elementary school doing a similar project.

Etcetera, etcetera, etcetera…

No better way to create real life connections than to create real life applications.

That's what makes learning so exciting – the art of possibilities. That's the relevance of connecting to real life.

+++++++

How does the material in this book connect to your real life?

Does it excite you?

How can you create that same experience for your learners?

Ch. 6. PREDICTABLE STRUCTURE

Predictability is related to safety. Thinking back to Maslow's Hierarchy, we are reminded that safety is the bottom of the pyramid, just above physiology:

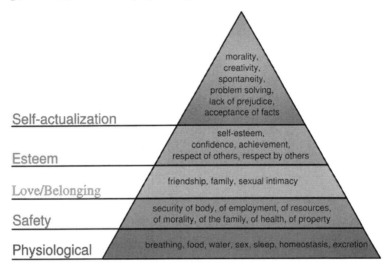

This is important to note because learning, as it relates to starting on the higher order thinking pyramid we identified in Chapter 3, doesn't happen until well into the Esteem level of Maslow. (That's in the middle.)

In order to provide a strong foundation on which to grow learning, the bottom of the pyramid needs to fill in as much as possible.

Don't misunderstand. It isn't that the needs represented in Maslow's Hierarchy have to be *perfectly* met to move up the pyramid. However, the more holes in the lower layers, the less solid the subsequent layers will be. Think about it with building blocks.

If there are holes in the bottom two or three layers, what happens as you build up? The stability is compromised.

There is always the opportunity to reinforce those bottom layers, however. In the picture above, a new tower was built reinforcing the first tower on the left hand corner. While there are still "holes" they are supported and reinforced in a way that they don't threaten the upper stability.

So it is with our learning experiences. By providing quality elements that ensure safety, the bottom of the pyramid is reinforced, regardless of home life or previous learning experience. The new, safe, learning environment creates a new "wing" on the foundational structure, reinforcing the upper learning. This makes learning easier.

Predictable structure in the classroom is one important component in learning because it is so connected to safety. Consistency is a large part of predictability. As a result, consistency is paramount.

That means as the learning leader the things I say, I do. When I establish habits and routines, they are the norm. When there is an interruption, I address it as just that; an interruption.

Predictability relates to safety and consequently to trust. Trust is one of the primary building blocks of relationships. Engagement is all about relationships.

I think this makes the importance of predictability clear.

Some of the challenges related to predictable structure include those predictable interruptions and those not-so-predictable interruptions. Predictable interruptions include days off, testing days, school wide activities, and emergency drills (to name a few). Unpredictable interruptions include absences (yours and theirs), behavior, or weather.

Part of predictable structure, however, is also built into your predictability of behavior as the learning leader. That means when there is an interruption for which there is time to prepare, you prepare your learners. For those that there is not the luxury of preparation, you explain as soon afterward as possible. This maintains the predictability, and thereby the trust, within the relationship.

Predictability in your behavior as the learning leader goes beyond interruptions though. For myself, I take great comfort and have great respect for those people whom I find predictable in their response to a given situation. I may not agree with them, but in knowing what to expect from them, there is an increase in my trust of them. This is related to congruency.

Congruency is, in this context, the match between what I say and what I do. It's directly related to consistency. For example, if I tell a group of learners, "It is important to me that everyone be able to understand what we are doing", I have to behave accordingly. Consequently, when I have a student or participant who raises a question for clarification, I do not respond in a way that is sarcastic or insulting.

Learner: "Can you explain number 2 again please?"

Leader: "Weren't you paying attention the first time?"

This type of response makes it unsafe – not only for this learner but others in the room – to ask questions related to something that has already been said.

A better response might be, "I'd be happy to. Do you need me to say it differently or did you just need me to repeat it the same way?"

This provides for an opportunity for the learner to ask for what they need in a more detailed manner. It also provides potential insight for the leader as to the learning process of that learner.

Reality is that I have found very few situations where that is the only learner with the issue. Most often, a question raised by one student is a reflection of more than just that student.

Another opportunity, of course, is to allow another student to explain, in this case, number two, again. Often times another perspective and use of language can help to increase understanding.

The bottom line is that when I say I support all learners and I want to ensure everyone understands what is being discussed, I need to be willing to act accordingly. That's congruity.

It seems logical here to discuss the myth of the "home life." In public education, there are often home life situations from which kids come that are less than optimal (yes, grossly understated!). As educators and learning leaders we cannot allow this to become an excuse for lack of engagement or lack of performance.

Instead we create a new template model. I have yet to find a kid of almost any age who is not able to understand the difference between one place and another, between grandma's house and mom's house, for example.

They can and do adapt their expectations and behaviors to each environment. It requires practice, to be sure! Yet with a little consistency and congruity the new habits and routines become the predictable and safe new environment.

Habits/routines + consistency + congruity = predictability.

Predictability = Safety.

This is stated simply. I know from my own experience that it is often way more complex to implement. I also know that time, consistency and congruity win. You have to apply perseverance.

In the end, there will be progress. Sometimes it is huge and obvious. Sometimes it is small and huge. Take note and take heart to them all.

+++++++

When it comes to predictability, what is your greatest strength?

Define and relate congruity and consistency, in your own words, to the concept of predictable structure.

What do you see as your area of weakness within this concept?

Ch. 7. MULTI-MODAL

Multi-modal is information presented in many different modalities. Modalities are ways we can take in information.

The primary modalities are the five senses; visual, auditory, kinesthetic, oral, and olfactory. Yet the concept of modalities is an expansion of those senses. I think of this like a Spirograph. Something really simple that becomes extremely complex.

While we have the foundational modalities in the senses, within each of those modalities are also a myriad of preferences. For example, while a learner may be auditory, their auditory preference may not be linguistic. That means that their strength in listening is potentially related to rhythm or auditory patterning and not necessarily to listening to words. Music, however, may be the perfect auditory medium for them compared to listening to lecture or reading out loud. Consequently, because learning environments are full of students with varied modalities and preferences within modalities, content needs to be multi-modal.

We all have our preferences *in* modality and *within* modality. Our preferences are the strong characteristics that, for example, show up in trait inventories (learning styles, communication, leadership, conflict, etc.). Be careful to remember these are measures of *preference*. They do not define who we are, but help to explain how we like to do things. There is quite a bit of research that indicates that preferences may not be the same across all content areas. I can be an auditory learner in language arts but a kinesthetic learner in science.

I raise this caution so that you clearly understand what preference inventories tell you and what they don't. This is important in how they are used most effectively.

As learning leaders, we have our own preferences which are often also our lead strengths. In short, our favorite way to teach is usually our favorite way to learn.

This is significant because I can guarantee that you will almost never have a room full of learners with your exact preferred modalities. Yet you are responsible to teach to all learners. It can present quite a conundrum!

Learning how to teach and present in ways that are somewhat challenging can be, well, a challenge. The first requirement is, of course, for you to know your preferences as a learner and a teacher. To obtain links to some inventories to get you started, see the Magic Resources.

Once you know your preferences, research everything you can about them. At the same time, read about all the other preferences. There are many activities in this book to help you along, just remember this is only the beginning. You are embarking on the lifelong journey of expanding who you are and who your students will become.

As you expand your own presentation styles, you will discover ways that support a variety of learners. In the best of all possible worlds, all important concepts are presented in as many modalities as possible.

Some examples from my own experience;

- K-3 inner city segregated special education classroom; We designed and created a "living" rain forest. With two of the largest tarps I could find, we duck taped three sides and most of the fourth. We had Velcro on the fourth side and a hole on the opposite side just big enough for a box fan. When the box fan was turned on, it inflated the tarps and created a space inside that the kids then got to create with trees, animals, vegetation, and flowers; and all the things they learned about that were in the rain forest. They had the opportunity to use the space during quiet reading time and free play. Almost every one of them could find a way to enjoy our rain forest. The exception included those students who couldn't handle the background noise from the box fan. They found it too distracting. While they participated in the learning and building, they seldom used it of their own choice.

I have used the same environment for astronomy and weather lessons with older students.

- K-5 multi-handicapped, self-contained classroom: We went on a "field trip" on the school grounds to identify and categorize all the trees we saw. They had to document their process either in writing or by voice recording, had a check list, and a partner. They were given the assignment and instructions before we left. They were able to choose how they presented their final report. Their choices included a panorama, a written report, or a sculpture. All of them had to provide an oral report (including the student who used an augmentative communication device).

- 7-9 World Language class (American Sign Language). A cultural report required research in 3 different modes; reading, listening, interviewing. They could choose their report delivery mode as spoken, written, or visual. It also had to provide at least one paragraph presented using American Sign Language. There were specific steps along the way, checked along the timeline. I had to provide a lot of the resources, especially for interviews, but the students enjoyed the full range.

- Adult professional development training workshop on diversity. The participants worked in groups to create a fully equitable town. They could choose to do it as a model, as a written representation, or in the form of a skit. Within the three-day experience we had identified learning and leading preferences and allowed them to group themselves with a level of awareness. The groups that had the most fun were those who had a variety of preferences represented in their membership. This was discussed in addition to their final projects.

You can see that, while it is important to provide plenty of opportunity for learners to stretch into their preferences, it is also important to find ways for success within their less preferred modalities. It is important for each of us to use ALL our muscles. The same is true for our modalities.

One word of caution. It is sometimes considered that there is "more" to learn through our weaker modalities than our strengths. After all, if you start at point A to get to point D there is more "growth" than if you start at point C to get to point D. However, when you consider the amount of time and energy required to get from point A to point D is so much greater than that from point C to point D, it is more likely that starting at point A will only get you to point B. Now there is a 2-letter gap between those who started at point A and those who started at point C. (Think about that the next time there is a discussion about the achievement gap or discipline disparities, but that's a different book!)

This exemplifies why multi-modal presentation is so important. It is one mechanism that can support bridging those diversities that tend to allow "gaps" to develop. It is a tool that can be used in culturally responsive education, full inclusion, and equal access classrooms.

+++++++

Have you learned your own preferences yet?

In my preferred presentation style, I use very general agendas that list topics but provide few details and no times. Feedback has informed me that this is a struggle for many participants. This has resulted in my fleshing out my agendas more and asking for permission from the group of learners to flex on the time. This compromise has seemed to work for most folks. What is an area of your preference that you know might (or does) challenge learners? How have your addressed it or how might you?

Ch. 8. MOVEMENT

Adding movement to the learning experience is one quick and easy way to increase engagement, decrease distraction, and increase attention. There is quite a bit of research that indicates that moving learners a minimum of every 10-30 minutes provides kids with what they need to keep their brains in the game. (Interested in the research? Check out the Magic Resources).

Movement can be incorporated into the learning experience through a variety of techniques. It can be intentional, separate from the content.

> "Okay, now I want you to stand up and stretch your arms over your head and take a big breath!"

Or it can be included as part of the learning experience.

> When there are short reading excerpts, they can be set up throughout the room so learners have to move from one to the other to read them. You can time the movements and include extra movement instructions in between the readings.

> "Okay, you've finished the first reading in the last 5 minutes. Now you're going to move to the next one, this time skip your way to the poster. You will have 7 minutes to skip to the poster and read. Then I will give the next set of instructions.

I think you can see that the possibilities are endless. Remember, everything we do is teaching p about how they learn and how they can optimize how, where, and what they learn. Low movement activities (indicated with an "L" in the following list) can help students even in the middle of a test or when restrictions are high. Larger movements can be utilized in the hallways during passing, helping kids prime themselves for the next set of expectations.

Here's a list to help get you going. This list isn't designed to be exhaustive. It's a launching point. What are your ideas??

1. (L) Hands open, palm to palm and push, gently.
2. (L)With your hands open, palm to palm, wiggle your fingers against each other. How fast can you go.
3. (L)With your index finger or first three fingers, tap the bone just below your neck right next to the "hole" that the collarbones make.
4. Trace your name with the finger of your non-dominant hand (the one you don't write with) on the desk/table in front of you. Try it in print and cursive.
5. (L) Relax your shoulders and drop your chin to your chest for a count of 5. Raise your head to look up, counting slowly to 5 and inhaling deeply. Lower it to your chest again, slowly counting to 5 and exhaling. Repeat 3 times.
6. Place your open palms on your thighs, left hand to left thigh, right to right. Switch hands so it is right hand to left thigh and left hand to right. Return and repeat 3 times.
7. Empty hands, then pick up your pencil, pen, or eraser. Pass it between your hands, back and forth as fast as you can for the count of 5. Try not to drop it.
8. Teacher hands out handwriting sheets and students write on them with their non-dominant hands.
9. On the desk or table in front of you, stretch your arms out forward and trace circles, first in the same direction and then in opposite directions.
10. Reach straight up with your left arm as high as you can with an inhale and quick exhale. Repeat with the right arm. Then try both arms at the same time.
11. Use a pencil, pen, or eraser and pass it between each of your fingers on one hand without the help of the other hand. Then switch and try it with the other hand.

12. Place one hand on the top of your head and the other on your stomach. Switch. Repeat. Now touch to your shoulders.

13. Have students stand up, behind their chair and use their chair to balance as needed, lifting first one leg straight behind them and then the other. Encourage a stretch with each leg.

14. Use the 1-2 chant to have fun as you prepare for quiet seat time. "1, 2 feet on the floor. 1, 2 hands in your lap. 1, 2 eyes on you. 1, 2 mouth goes shut."

15. When passing out papers, use it as an opportunity for movement. Have the students moving as fast as they can to get the papers passed out to everyone while you count. Set goals for rewards of extra time to chat with a neighbor at the end of class or work toward a class reward.

16. Have students stand up and move to the chair to their left. They then sit down. Stand up and move to the chair to their right. Sit down. They are now in their own chair but it gave them a chance to move.

17. When students are getting "squirrelly" or just coming from a high energy activity, use the 10 second wiggle to help them transition. Set a timer or count to ten as they wiggle their whole bodies as much as they can. With practice, this can become a game of returning to order fastest with lots of opportunity for praise.

18. Provide stress balls, small slinkies, or other such toys - one per student. The rules are 1) it can't disrupt your learning 2) it can't disrupt anyone elses' learning, and 3) if it hits the floor you lose it for that subject or class period. This provides students with a "fidget" toy to be able to move at will. Some teachers have to teach themselves to ignore the movement and allow their students to attend to their own needs.

19. Stretch out your hands in front of you. Wiggle your fingers as fast as you can. Stretch at the shoulders and take a deep breath. Repeat as needed.

20. (L) Place open palm of right hand on front of left shoulder and open palm of left hand on right shoulder. Pat gently.
21. Have students stand and do jumping jacks or running in place to the count of ten. Usually this is more effective if it is followed by a lower energy movement to help them transition.
22. (L) While seated, place right and left hand on right hip. Hold for the count of five. Switch so both hands are now on the left hip. Hold for the count of five. Repeat as desired.
23. (L) Pull shoulders back, trying to get the scapula (shoulder blades) to touch. This usually will elicit a yawn as it opens the chest cavity.
24. (L) Teaching students to deep breath is a life-long skill. Have them breathe in slowly through their nose, filling first their belly and then their chest. Have them hold for a slow count of 3 and then exhale through their mouth with a sharp release and then a count of 3. You can encourage sighing noises!
25. Have students clap their hands together and then clap their hands to their opposite shoulders (right hand on front of left shoulder, left hand on front of right shoulder).

+++++++

What have you used to increase movement in your learning environment?

What do you do when your brain starts to space out during a learning experience?

I'd love to hear any additions to the list! leah@with-respect.com

Ch. 9. FROM HERE…

The big picture goal of this book is that it provides a concrete explanation of engagement with the how's and why's clearly delineated. Part 2 is all about activities that directly implement what has been discussed in Part 1. The ultimate goal is that, Parts 1 and 2 provide you with what you need to adopt, adapt, and create from the activities in this book.

Explore your relationship with your learners.

As a classroom teacher, teacher aide, administrator or other child educator, you have opportunities to create meaningful relationships with kids that have impacts you may not even begin to imagine.

As a trainer or speaker, don't underestimate the impact the relationships you create also have on individuals and organizations.

As an executive or other leader in an organization, you have the ability to impact and support lifelong relationships for employees and customers – with each other, the organization, themselves, and their communities.

Engagement is amazing and powerful!

I have had the privilege of experiencing that first hand. I continue to have those I have had as young students, colleagues, employees, and adult students circle back around to tell me the positive influence I provided – in something I said or did that I never thought twice about.

That's the gift of being a learning leader. It's a privilege that comes with responsibility. Perhaps the largest responsibility , and greatest privilege, is to engage with each learner.

That's where we go from here; continuing our journey, the Magic of Engagement.

Part 2.

ACTIVITES:

THE WHAT
OF ENGAGEMENT

Classroom Rules.	**IB**

When:

I've classified this activity as an "in-between" (IB) mostly because it is something that works across the classroom, a foundation, a culture builder. It could just as easily be classified as a "before" (B) because in order for it to work you have to have done it ahead of time, before content delivery. At the same time, it could be classified as a "during" (D) since the use of it is during class time and content delivery as well as all the in-between times. As you will see, for many of the activities timing is a little fluid, but for the sake of simplicity, you will see the classification of each in the location above. If you have any confusion about why something is what it is, contact me and we can discuss it.

Prep Time: Nominal time is required if materials are used and re-used. Class time requires about 10 min. daily for about 2 weeks.

Materials: Rules printed out with pictures, movements chosen. For Leah's choice, see Magic Resources.

Description:

Classroom rules are used to provide structure, consistency, common language, common expectations, and a sense of order to the classroom. Utilized as outlined here, they serve to build relationships and community as well as provide a strong foundation to classroom management.

Classroom rules are foundational in a classroom. The more emphasis we place on them as leaders in the classroom, the more useful they become. Simplicity is important. So is repetition. They need to become part of the lifeblood of the classroom. Every student needs to know them as part of their own breath. The best way I've learned to do this is through call and response with an added gesture. This comes directly out of brain development and cultural responsiveness research. I have traditionally used 3 to 5 rules.

For today, it's 4. I teach these by first reading them to the class. (The visuals for this set of rules is included in the appendix). We talk about examples of each one and what they mean, concretely. Then I teach a gesture for each one that the students emulate. The first one, index finger points to the chest. Then I say, "Repeat after me and copy my movements (which are of course, the ones I'm teaching them). Rule #1, respect myself." The students repeat it back.

The second one the index finger sweeps out, across the group. And I say, "Repeat after me with the gesture, Rule #2 respect others." The students respond.

The third one, I sweep the room with an open palm facing up and say "Rule #3, respect property." The students repeat it.

The fourth one, I touch my index finger to my temple and say "Rule #4 ask clarifying questions." Students repeat.

I then do this every day for a week, then fade off. It gets to the point that I can ask the class or any individual student "what's rule #3" and they can automatically respond.

This is important as a tool because then when there is an infraction I use the rules, couched with peer support, to address behaviors. Let's say I have a blurter; Johnny is a student who just can't keep his mouth from opening with the answer or a smart remark. This is a direct offense to rule #2, respect others. So it happens. I turn to the class and say, "Class what's rule #2?" They respond in unison. Looking at Johnny, I remind him, "blurting out is disrespectful to others." I then move on with what I'm doing. If it happens a second time, I now ask Johnny directly, "What's rule #2?" He responds. I then ask what an alternative or the expected behavior is and wait for the response. If he has any trouble, I ask the class or a classmate to help him come up with something.

If it happens a third time, I now know that the issue is either related to a disability (quote unquote) or discipline. In this way,

I have reduced the likelihood that the issue is related to a cultural oversight or conflict. Johnny has had the opportunity to understand his behavior as outside of the expectations and been given alternatives. Now, it may be obvious that Johnny is making an effort and just needs practice. As the one in charge, I can make that call and find ways to support Johnny. I especially praise him when he does well.

Classroom Rules utilized this way build community, establish expectations of behavior, and allow students to support and regulate themselves and each other. They become self-managers. That means as the one in the front of the room, I have to referee less. There is more time for teaching. The environment is one that supports the full array of learners. We all have more room to have fun. It also lays the groundwork to be able to manage conflicts, confusion, and bad days.

I think you get the picture of how useful this can be for a classroom teacher, a small group that meets consistently, a training environment, or even at home as a parent.

Strategies.

Relationship Building. This activity helps to establish the room climate by making the expectations of behavior and interaction very clear. It gives foundations for language that can be used within and across relationships and in the building of community. By establishing and consistently implementing the classroom rules, fairness and predictability are inherent in the environment. This provides for safety in the learning environment and encourages students to be willing to take risks within themselves, with each other, and with academic content.

Predictable Structure. The consistency of use of the classroom rules helps to establish equity and fairness and the predictability that consistency fosters.

Movement. The gestures used to teach, reinforce, and recall the classroom rules is an example of the support movement provides learning by allowing the content of the concepts to become part of the community and individual thinking. As discussed in the Movement and Multi-Modal Chapters earlier in the book, movement is part of the multi-modal approach.

Variations.

There's not much I can recommend about variations to this activity. There are variations within it, however.

Regardless if what you are doing is one on one, small groups, classrooms, or auditoriums, rules are important in one form or another to begin to build a relationship. What you call them, what they are, how you use them is different. The importance is in the fact that you have them and use them, that they are part of the full picture.

The rules and gestures can vary. It is recommended that the rules be simple – no more than a few words each – and that the set (total number of rules) not exceed five. This allows them to be usable and flexible.

I've used the first three rules forever in every environment. If you've ever been in a class, training, or workshop with me you know that I use these three rules consistently. I sometimes include a few additions STRETCH (getting folks outside their comfort zone which is where we learn) and ENJOY (since we know people remember more when they are having fun.)

Additionally, I use an acronym to define respect.

Respect is one of those words we throw around like we all mean the same thing. Yet we also know it has cultural, experiential, personal, and familial connotations that vary from one person to another. It is for that exact reason that I use my acronym. Remember Empathy Sincerity Patience Equity Courtesy/ Compassion Truthfulness.

You can create your own acronym and/or allow classes to create their own as a community. Either way I find the concept of the acronym gives something to hang your hat on; it provides a concrete idea of what is meant by the word.

FYI: Using the acronym as a vocabulary builder is a way to bridge the concept of your classroom community into your content as well.

Regardless, this helps to make the first three rules cover any infraction that can occur. It gives more information for reference to a behavior. Remember Johnny our blurter? I can expand on the reason why blurting is disrespectful by reminding Johnny that as a community we know that we need to be patient and courteous so others have a chance to respond as well. That way we have also provided a foundation for alternative behaviors that show respect.

Guidelines	IB

The Four Agreements

Description:

First, it is best if you read the book, <u>The Four Agreements</u> by don Miguel Ruiz. It's worth your time. I've read and

<u>Prep Time</u>: Nominal time is required if materials are used and re-used. Class time requires about 10 min. daily for about 2 weeks.

<u>Materials</u>: The Four Agreements printed out. See Magic Resources

re-read it more than 50 times and I still learn stuff every time.

Remember, they are the FOUR agreements, not the agreement of the day. They work together to create the foundation of language and conversation and relationships within myself and my communities.

The Four Agreements are pretty simple and straightforward. You can't have missed them if you have EVER been in a training, work group, or other experience with me. This is my typical introduction of them.

Agreement 1. Be impeccable with your word.

Think of Dr. Seuss's <u>Horton Meets a Who</u>: "I say what I mean and mean what I say". Pretty simple, right? Yes, until you realize that it means *all the time*. It means those things you say out loud and those you say inside yourself; those things you say to others and those things you say to yourself. If I wouldn't call you stupid (and I wouldn't), I don't call me stupid. You can see how powerful this simple agreement can be for you as an individual, for a class as a community, for people over all.

It's about consistency and congruence. If I tell you I will do something, I do it. This agreement has caused me to consider what I say, to who, and how. For example, my two children were to clean their room, given an hour to complete the task. They were 3 and 4. I told them that when they were done, any toys left out and not where they belonged would go into a bag and we would give them to other children who didn't have so many toys.

During the hour, my 3-year old son sat on his bed with his coloring book the whole time. I poked my head in a couple times and reminded him. He always smiled and said, "Ok!"

The hour was up and walked into his room with a plastic shopping bag. Nothing had been done. He looked at me and said, "That bag's not big enough." I had no choice but to follow through on what I had said.

That's why I always remember that I have to be fully aware of what I say and be willing to do, be, or say whatever I have spoken. I can assure you I am much more careful about my words!

The cool thing is that my relationships reflect it. My family and friends know that not only do I say what I mean and do what I say, but I won't agree to things I don't believe or am not willing to do.

Imagine what THAT can do in the classroom! It eliminates the excuse of "just kidding" that often follows hurtful words or actions. It challenges the ideas of gossiping (a challenge across the agreements). It makes us think before we speak, inside and out.

Now, impeccable is a big word. I've used The Four Agreements with kids as young as 3 years old in preschool classrooms. I've explained the word in ways that are developmentally appropriate and clear. The result? Nothing is cuter than one 3-year old saying to another, "You're not being 'peccable!" and using it exactly when and where it should be used. Teach it so they understand. Catch them doing it and use the word. Point out when it isn't being applied and give examples of how it would look if it were. That's how we improve working vocabulary, right?

Agreement 2. Don't make assumptions.

I translate this into communicate, communicate, communicate.

As humans, in the absence of data we create data. Think about when you know only a few details of a story and the tales you can spin in your head and the complexity and depth... Then you find out the reality and it's not half as good as what your imagination created! That's what assumption does, it fills in for the information that is missing. Typically, this is not a good thing.

For example, I pass you in the hall and you don't make eye contact or growl at me. I can assume that you are mad at me, that I've done something that really ticked you off, or that you're just a real somethin'-somethin' and get angry myself.

Or.

I can stop you and ask what's up and if you're all right. I can engage in a quick check in to be sure that our relationship is okay. I might ask if you need to catch coffee together at the next break or if it would be okay to talk over lunch.

I also don't second guess your intentions. If you say, "I'm okay. Just deep in thought. Thanks for asking." I believe you and don't keep writing a script that says, "I know there's more to that story. I bet he just got some really bad news and doesn't want to talk about it."

Communicate, communicate, communicate.

Think, now, of how this could apply in the classroom. It encourages questioning for understanding and open communication and genuine interest. It invites communication through questions instead of statements, inquiry instead of judgment. It has application for content, community, conflict, and communication.

Agreement 3. Don't take things personally.

THE MAGIC OF ENGAGEMENT

This is a big one.

We are all the star of our own movie. The rest of you are just extras in my script. The only experience and perspective I have is mine. I don't know what I don't know. All of these are true and reinforce why it is so important to not take things personally.

The Four Agreements came into my life when my youngest son was four years old. I wasn't sure I was going to be able to raise him. He would later go on to be diagnosed with a mood disorder that was contributing but our family dynamics weren't helping. This agreement made the whole difference in our lives and relationship.

Don't take it personally. It gave me permission and perspective that when he screamed, "I hate you!" and would throw himself at me in a blind rage I could remember it was all about him, in that moment. It wasn't about me. It gave me the tools to be able to say, "I hear you... and when you are done, I will still love you and hold you." It meant I didn't have to do anything, I didn't have to escalate with him. I just held the space while he worked himself through it. When it was over, we could hug, have a meaningful conversation and move on without resentment, fear, or anger. It was *huge*.

The catch-phrase in our household that grew from this agreement was "that's so about you." It was the reminder between and among us that the behavior that was happening belonged to the behaver, not the behavees. The 'star' and the 'extras' were identified and could settle into their roles.

What happens when you empower children with tools to understand seemingly irrational behavior? They become your greatest reflectors.

One day, I walked in the door from a frazzled day at work and, for whatever reason, I blew up at the kids and ranted for quite a few minutes. My then 7-year old son put his hands on his hips, looked me square in the eye and said, "That is so about you!"

And he was right. I immediately acknowledged his wisdom and sent myself to my room for a 10 minute time out. When I was done, there was no damage done on either side and we moved forward in the evening routine. What a gift!

This is a powerful tool for us as adults to use and to empower kids to use. In creating respectful communities we also need to respect when they are right – with themselves, each other, and us.

Agreement 4. Do your best all the time.

This is *not* an excuse for those of us who are overachievers to beat ourselves up.   It is a way to understand that every moment our best looks a little different. If I've had a full night's sleep, the sun is shining, and I'm feeling great my best looks a lot different than if I was up half the night with a sick baby, it's raining outside, and I have the flu.

It is the opportunity to remember that we all are doing the best we can with what we've got in any given moment. If that best isn't meeting an expectation then there is one of three things missing; information, skills, or resources. Keep in mind that resources can be anything from enough sleep to maturity.

Within the classroom or community this provides foundations for accountability and meeting expectations. It allows for the accountability of doing our best while understanding that there are things that impact our best and thus our performance. In so doing we give room for praise and growth as well as room for error and improvement.

Strategies.

Relationship Building. Guidelines are foundational in establishing relationships, how we talk to one another, what the expectations are within our interactions, and conversations, as well as the glue that holds things together when the road gets a little tough. The Four Agreements go a long way in creating that foundation when introduced and applied.

Predictable Structure. When a community, whether 2 or 2000, agrees to guidelines and actively uses them, everything becomes predictable. The cool thing about The Agreements is that even when difficult conversations and conflicts happen, the guidelines are there to pave the way.

Variations.

I raised my kids using The Four Agreements. I've used them in classrooms, school systems, and in my business. That means they are flexible in one on one situations, small groups, varied cultures, and with large groups. There isn't much that is required to change. Most importantly, the introduction, conversation, and implementation needs to be developmentally appropriate while pushing the development forward.

The Four Agreements are not a mastered skill; they are an evolution of self and group interaction. I encourage you to read the book (it's a little book, quick read, deep content) and talk with others about their perspective, use, and engagement with the text. In my experience, it has the potential to be the most life changing component of what we do. I have several people, including my own children and dear colleagues, who speak to the depth and breadth that this little book has allowed them to go.

Call & Response IB

(Get their attention)

Description:

The idea of call and response is far from new. It has been used as a culturally responsive technique as well as just for the logic and ease of getting students' attention. It's the idea that as the leader I say something, and the class as a unit says something back.

| Prep Time: Need to teach the students the technique. With older students and adults, they can catch on without any intro.

Materials: None. |

The goal and purpose is a polite way to bring students together, to get their attention. I use it at the beginning of class, when I'm ready for them to return to the large group when they have been working individually or in small groups or anytime I kind of lose control. Using it with the idea of a warning system is helpful. It's a respectful way to say, "Finish what you're doing so I can talk to you." For that reason, the objective is not abject obedience. It's more like a gentling.

When setting it up with students, I start with something expected, I actively teach the call and response I will use. It would go like this:

Leader: "I say come on you say back. Come on"

Students: "Back"

Leader: "Come on"

Students: "Back"

Leader: "Come on"

Students: "Back"

Generally, the call and response occurs three times. This is the gentling. It gives students a chance to gather themselves and focus their attention on you with a deadline but a little bit of grace. The entire class should be participating by the third response.

It's fun and important to mix it up, too. Sometimes it might be more like, "I say mac, you say cheese" or "I say pirates, you say arrg." Variety keeps it interesting and allows for a need for the students to pay attention.

Additionally, you can allow students to be the leader in certain situations where they might need to get the attention of their peers. For example, the line leader might need to get the students attention to line up or if they are presenting to the class might have a need to refocus their peers. Encourage students to play with it.

Lastly, allowing for student suggestions that they place in a jar that you can pull out randomly and use is always fun for everyone. This is another layer of community building within the classroom.

Strategies.

Relationship Building. The level of respect and clarity of expectation provided by this simple activity goes a long way in relationship building and nurturing.

Multi-Modal. By utilizing the listening and speaking this activity becomes multi-modal. It can also incorporate movement by utilizing, "I say hoo, you say ray" and incorporate a raised fist from shoulder to the air on the "ray."

Predictable Structure. By establishing the expectation and what happens, by whom, and when, the predictability is clear within the structure.

Variations.

    1. Leader: "1-2-3 eyes on me."
           Students: "1-2 eyes on you."

This one is said only once and is often used when the response needs to be quicker. This might be because something is happening that needs to be interrupted like two students squaring off. It might also be done as a redirection if students get off task and need to be reminded what they are supposed to be doing.

2. Leader: "Clap once if you can hear me."
   Students clap once.
   Leader: "Clap twice if you can hear me"
   Students clap twice.
   Continue increasing the number of claps until you have all students' attention. This can become a competition with themselves to see how quickly they can refocus as a community. "Wow! That was so much better than last time. Good job!"

3. Leader: "Come together in 5-4-3-2-1"
   The goal is that the students focus on you by the time you get to one. This is particularly useful in situations where there might be a lower keyed tone, or you just had them working individually. It's great for wrapping up testing time or for in-between time – that time moving from one subject to another or from an activity like passing out papers. You can vary the pace of the countdown to accommodate as needed. It can be slow if you need to give a student or two the chance to catch up or the pace can increase if they are all ready sooner.

Check In/Out   IB

Description:

Checking in and out with students is an opportunity to connect with them at a much deeper level, regardless of how many of them there are.

I have used check in and check out when I taught American Sign Language with high school students. I had almost 100 students, and it was the only way I could come up with to connect with each one of them in a meaningful way.

Prep Time: Based on choices. Most require some use of prompts – paper, cards, etc. but it doesn't have to; you can make it up in your head and have them write it on a sheet of notebook paper. That simple.

Materials: There are example of check-in and check-out sheets as well as the 'what's on your mind' cards in Magic Resources.

I set up a file folder for each student with their name on the tab and put each period into a separate hanging file box. Inside each one was a check-in sheet that asked for two pieces of information: "Name" and "How are you today?"

There was also a check out sheet asking them if they knew what the homework was, when the next test was and if they understood what we discussed today. It also asked for anything else they wanted to tell me.

Lastly, any handout for that day's class was also in the file folder.

They could choose to answer the questions any way they chose, but they had to write something. "Fine" or the equivalent was acceptable to answer how they were today. Yes and no worked for the check out.

Most students chose to write much more. The depth and breadth of their sharing was amazing. I learned who was considering suicide, who just broke up with their girl/boy-friend, whose grandmother had just been diagnosed with cancer, who was struggling with the class, with me, or with a classmate.

It required I read through the whole stack of folders each night. It was time consuming, but it was worth it! The relationships I had with all of those students was amazing. Their level of loyalty and willingness was huge. Even those students, whom other teachers found challenging, did well socially and academically in my class.

Some of the students tested me to see if I was reading them. They'd give me a line like "Mary had a little lamb" to which I responded "It's fleece was white as snow." I had one student who would start jokes and knock-knocks with me. It was great fun for me as well.

Students also turned in their homework in their folders which gave it a bit more of a private feel for them. It also meant that if it was missing it was noticeable to me. It gave me the opportunity to follow up with them one on one about it.

Overall, the relationships were awesome. Many of those students still see me in our community, give me a hug, and catch me up on their lives. I still remember their names and many of our private jokes.

But it doesn't have to be that elaborate. You can do check-ins once a week or as a "surprise quiz." Just a way to touch base and check the pulse of your students. Talk about your expectations before you ever hand them one, but use them as much as you can. Use them to check-in about the class work, the climate, the culture, or their holiday. Whatever you'd like to know more about.

Check-outs I've always used as the pulse of the work for today. I have used them as "exit slips," meaning you can't leave until you turn one in. You can use the check-out for informal formative assessment. It's a way to gauge whether they are following, particularly when the content is foundational and something that will need to be built on as the information moves forward.

There's no reason that the check in or out has to be on paper. In adult trainings I've been known to toss a ball around the room and have each person share the most impactful thing they learned.

Similarly, in my classrooms I've used the ball as a contest element. The person who has the ball is asked a question from the content and attempts to answer. In the event they don't know the answer, they can throw the ball to a classmate as their lifeline. That means the person tells them the answer, throws the ball back, and they repeat the response. This is a great reinforcement for the concept as well.

Strategies:

Relationship Building. I think you can see how this contributes to the relationship building.

Predictable Structure. Check-ins and check-outs allow students to know what to expect regarding their ability to retain and respond with material as well as the consistency of their use. This is why it matters less what intervals they are used and more about the consistency of their use.

Connect to Real Life. Based on how you use them, check-ins and check-outs can help students make the connections between the classroom and the real world. Certainly the way I used the check-ins allowed students to bring their lives into the classroom on a consistent basis without it becoming any type of drama.

Variations.

There are many variations discussed above including the use of file folders and exit slips. There is also the "What's on your mind" cards. These can be used on Friday afternoons, following a test, or other times there might be a little extra time. You draw a card (you can make them or have the students help you) and have the students volunteer their response. The questions might be "Given today's assignment/test, how are you feeling about your performance in this class and why?"

Responses aren't required but respect is mandatory for anyone who chooses to answer. You can also have the students write their response and choose to share out loud or not. Then you can collect them and have the ability to do a little more monitoring.

Another variation is a "Chat Circle." This is like circle time in elementary classes, though there is no age restriction. These are quite useful around holidays or school-wide testing when the schedule gets a little wonky and kids need a little more regrouping. Using them as class meetings to address issues among/within/ and around what might be happening in the class (good or bad) can also be useful.

Brain Connectors | IB

Prep Time: None really.

Materials: for variations you may need handwriting sheets printed out, large paper, sidewalk chalk, markers, etc.

Description:

People get sleepy, zoned out, and squirrelly when their brains disconnect – literally.

By helping kids (and adults) reconnect the left and right hemispheres of their brain <u>and</u> connect their brain to their body, you improve their ability to pay attention and stay engaged.

Doing that is simple: Brain Connectors.

Have the students stand (though it can be done seated) and plae their hands on their shoulders; right to right and left to left.

Then have them move their hands to their thighs; right to left and left to right.

Now back to the shoulders; right to left and left to right.

Back to their thighs; right to right and left to left.

Finally, to the shoulders; right to right and left to left.

That's it. You're done. The order of what comes when isn't even important. The goal is to have them cross the midline of their body. In this way the two sides of the brain connect. The movement reconnects the body and the brain.

Pretty simple, eh?

Strategies:

Multi-modal because it's kinesthetic (and auditory)

Movement because they're moving.

Variations:

1.   Off-Hand Writing. Print handwriting sheets and have students trace them with their non-dominant hand. It's fun, quick, and it helps to connect both sides of their brain and re-engage them.

2.   Double Scribble. Have kids draw giant figure-8's with both hands at the same time. It's important to cross the midline of their bodies. It can be large paper on their desk or a table or in midair without any writing implement. It can also happen where sidewalk chalk can be used like on the playground or a chalkboard. It even works with whiteboards and dry erase markers

3.   Hand Press. Have students place their hands, palm to palm, in front of their chest and press against each other, elbows out. Have them take three big breaths and count to ten. That's all. The contact between both palms and the pressure helps to connect the brain hemispheres and the big breath and counting re-focuses their mind.

Comment Box IB

Description:

While we are all familiar with comment boxes, in a classroom environment they require explanation, clear expectations and feedback.

Prep Time: Set up requires putting out the box and papers. Follow up requires reading the papers and responding.

Materials: a box with a slot. Papers with or without print.

Setting it up is the easy part. Any box with a slot in the top or side will work. Then set up the papers. The papers can have prompts written on them or not, based on the context of the comments. Consider if they are about the classroom, content, a specific activity, relationships, etc.

A discussion is required. This should be a lesson in writing respectful, constructive suggestions and criticisms as well as learning how to give appropriate praise. Discuss if there are prompts on the paper. They might include "What I like about my classroom" and "What I don't like about my classroom."

I have always used a comment box in a finite amount of time. There is a deadline. I use it for a specific purpose; to get feedback about something new we have tried in the classroom or if there is a relational dynamic happening that can be addressed better with anonymity.

For example, I had a situation where there was a shift in the classroom that was resulting in, what looked like, ganging up on one student. It was impacting the community and sense of safety within the classroom. I decided to use the comment box, set up over a full week, to get some insight. The prompts read "Name one thing that has changed about our classroom dynamics in the last couple weeks" and "What has been your contribution to that change" and "What are your feelings about that change?"

The long and the short of it was that there had been a falling out between two good friends who were prominent leaders in the classroom. EVERYONE knew it. Ironically, I didn't have to do anything about it. Raising the awareness of the community allowed the community to address it among and within themselves. By the time the comment box was removed, the situation was resolved.

Don't think, however, that the comment box is only for use for complaint or concern. It is also well advised within a system to give opportunity and place for learners to express their celebrations and happy thoughts.

In the initial discussion of the comment box, the parameters need to be clear. If using it incidentally (as opposed to constantly) then clarity will be even more important.

Strategies:

Relationship Building. This supports the idea that what students have to say is important and will be considered; important concepts within relationships.

Predictable Structure. When used consistently, this can be one of those practices that are trusted to be available for conflict and concern as well as for compliment and celebration.

Variations:

Many variations have been discussed above, looking at positive and negative feedback. Further variations can include:

Feedback Conferences. This is an opportunity to use comment boxes for individuals instead of systems. I have used it most often as a feedback mechanism for student presentation. Students provide critiques of their classmates' presentations on a form with their signature. There is then a chance for students to engage with one another in a conference to discuss the feedback – celebration and criticism – to deepen the experience for both parties. This means that the one providing the critique needs to have clarity in what they write so they can expand on it. This is an example of the executive order processes of evaluation and analysis.

Daily Feedback. This is what I have used in multi-day trainings to identify what is working and what is not working about how I have set up the learning experience and content. It can easily be expanded to work within a classroom, particularly for concepts and lessons that expand across several days.

Paper Race!	IB

Description:

Distributing papers, whether handouts or materials, is one of those times when disruption and mayhem can ensue. Somehow it

Prep Time: Other than teach time, none.

Materials: Just the papers to be distributed.

often becomes license for chatting and social discourse. By utilizing an engagement strategy not only do you minimize the distractibility of learners, but it helps to get it done more quickly.

In the Paper Race students are racing against themselves, as a community. So the goal is to do better today than yesterday, better this afternoon than this morning, etc. Rules require that everyone remains in their seat but must pass the papers as quickly as possible. There's a timer involved that is triggered by the first "carrier" who begins the timer at the same time as begins the distribution. Depending on the set up, there may need to be a runner from one table to another and then there is always the final runner who brings whatever is left over to the front of the room and stops the timer. The time is recorded and speed noted. As the leader, you can also set the time expectation.

"I bet you can do this in under 1 minute!"

For many students the challenge is a welcome motivator.

Strategies:

Relationship Building: It takes team work to do it quickly and respectfully.

Predictable Structure: Knowing that as a community we are working to do the mundane as quickly as possible is an important component to climate and culture. Additionally, it allows the community to self-manage.

Movement: The action itself, even just a twist in a chair to hand it to the neighbor behind or beside you is a movement that allows blood flow and shifts focus.

Variations:

File Folders. As I explained early in part one, I have used individual file folders to deliver the lesson materials on a daily basis. When I provide handouts to training participants, I often do it with a folder with all the needed materials.

Paper Countdown. This is another variation of the race where the leader picks a number and counts backwards. The goal is for all the papers to be distributed by the time 0 is called. This works really well with small groups and inclusion classrooms where a little stretch might be necessary to guarantee success. It might be to slow waaaaay down. So there is ample opportunity for someone who needs a little extra time to move.

Assigned Roles. This is a more traditional classroom management tool where there are assigned jobs in the classroom. Those jobs can rotate daily or weekly. There can still be a challenge of distractibility for the remaining students depending on the climate and culture.

Student-Teacher Conference | IB

Description:

Creating the time for one on one conferencing with students is a luxury. If it can be arranged, it should. All you need is 10 minutes per student. It can be carved out during times like silent reading time or project work time. It can also be included as part of Rotational Instruction (pg. 89).

Prep Time: You will need to prepare the response form from your perspective.

Materials: Response forms for both the teacher and the student. Samples and copies in Magic Resources.

Conferences are used for a specific purpose. I have always designed them for one assignment or, in the case of behavior challenges, one behavioral goal. The clear focus increases the likelihood it can be managed in a short time. They are not necessarily designed as something only done at the end of the experience. Particularly with multi-stepped projects, I have often used conferences at intervals throughout the assignment. I find it helps keep students on track a little better. I don't grade for the conference. It does, however, play into the final grade. When I make suggestions, I expect to see them considered. That doesn't guarantee they are included, but the conferencing along the way will make the consideration clear.

There are two paper forms; one for the teacher and one for the student. The questions are generally the same for each person with changes for the perspective. They are different, of course, for assignments versus behavior. The commonality is on teacher assessment of student's performance and student assessment of student performance. Note, though, that the student also has an opportunity to assess the teacher's role from their perspective. This provides feedback for both sides about what works and doesn't work within this learning relationship.

Strategies:

Relationship Building. Meaningful conversation builds relationships. Being able to listen and be heard also adds to the respect and meaningfulness of the relationship.

Predictable Structure. Used as a tool with consistency, particularly across an assignment, it becomes one more way in which response and reflection are supported in a predictable, safe manner.

Multi-Modal. The mechanism allows for the writing, speaking, and listening.

Variations:

There are lots of ways this can be varied just by the nature of the activity. Here are a couple considerations, particularly for individuals with varying abilities and disabilities.

Video/Audio Recording. The recording replaces the paper form. This can be useful in that it provides a varied way of recording the information as well as allowing for the information exchange to happen outside of the classroom. This can be particularly useful if behavior is being discussed or if there is a constraint on time available for the conference. The important consideration, however, is how it will become a conference and not another delivery of an assignment.

Pic-report. Utilizing pictures, whether drawn or cut out and pasted from another source, is another way to complete the feedback form. This will require conversation and is often a favorable mechanism that can include great depth. Words can be limiting for some individuals. Pictures open new doors for new ways to discuss.

Learn Their Names	B

Prep Time: None.

Materials: perhaps supplies for making name tags, index cards for your notes.

Description:

I don't think the concept needs much explaining after all "learn their names" is pretty straight forward. However, there are some tricks and tips that can help you (and them) remember all their names (yes, even when you have 7 different classes with 30 kids all in one day). Name tags are <u>always</u> helpful for the first few weeks of class. Don't forget to learn how to say their names as well.

I have a challenging last name to pronounce (Key – ā – ō). My daughter attended a small liberal arts college for her bachelor's program. When she graduated, even with cue cards, they didn't pronounce her name correctly. Not cool! Did not lead me to believe that they cared about her as an individual.

Names are the first layer of our self-identity. Calling me by my given and/or preferred name goes a long way in creating a meaningful relationship between us. It helps me to know that you care who I am, not just that I am a name on your roster who happens to be present.

That said, it's not always easy. Here are some suggestions to help the process along.

1. Play icebreaker games that emphasize names (try an internet search "icebreakers to learn people's names"). Use them for the first 10 minutes of every class for about a week. Try a different one every day!
2. Learn one row/table/section of the room at a time.
3. Have the students help by saying their name every time they speak or you point to them. Make it fun! Maybe they can sing their names one day.

4. Correlate names to noticeable attributes – things that aren't likely to change. Amy has cute chubby angel cheeks. Ryan is a runner. You get the idea.

5. For students with the same names (2 Joshes, 4 Taylors, etc.) have them determine who's who. Stay away from numbering them and you certainly don't want anything that is seen or felt to have a negative connotation. There is also nothing wrong with simply using the first letter of their last name when possible.

6. Find out if there are any stories associated with their names. Encourage kids to find out from home and share why their names were chosen. Share your own story. Do this with an awareness that this can be an area that is painful for some whose home lives or birth circumstances are different or difficult. It's not a reason to avoid the activity and may be the perfect way to have difficult conversation safely within a community.

Strategies.

Relationship Building. In order to build relationships, you have to know their names.

Variations.

Regardless of group size or anything else, you have to know their names.

Trait Inventories   B

Description.

Everyone loves to learn about themselves. That's what trait inventories do; they provide information about what individual learning style, communication style, and conflict style you prefer. They also correlate your personality to colors and letters and give you a list of things like your varied intelligences, what side of your brain you use and what impact your birth order might have on your relationships.

Prep Time: Depending on what inventories you will use, need time to take and score your own, know how to administer, score, and share the results.

Materials: Inventories and scoring sheets (list of potential web resources in Magic Resources).

As group leaders and educators we are also interested in the group dynamics are present. Knowing that the majority of my class is visual learners will influence how I present certain types of information. Recognizing that the room is split between extroverts and introverts means I need to balance out the opportunities for needs to be met. The potential for the use of inventories is limitless. The bonus is that most people like to take them!

Learning style preference, for instance, is something useful for each of us to understand about ourselves. When I know that I am a visual, linguistic learner I know that my preference for information is in pictures with language attached. I now have a set of tools that I look for in the presentation of information. I can ask for what I need from instructors. More importantly, I can also learn how to compensate for myself when information isn't presented in my preference or when I find myself confused. I can learn to draw pictures, talk about it with friends, or draw graphs and charts.

Looking at my place within my class can help me to see who my "like-minded" learners might be as well as giving me an idea of how many I am. Does the class have lots of learners like me or am I one of a few?

As the instructor, I can look at a room of learners and understand how to present information in multiple ways for multiple preferences. I can also begin to formulate how to help students learn through their weaker traits. For example, that visual, linguistic learner might benefit from listening to text being read (reinforcing auditory linguistic) or creating pictures without words to explain a process or concept (reinforcing visual creative).

This is just an example of how trait inventories can inform classroom and instructional design. As educators and leaders our expectations are that our students learn first about themselves and second about themselves in the world. Trait inventories help us to do that.

Strategies.

Relationship Building. When we learn about ourselves within a community we have the opportunity to come to a clearer understanding of who "I" am and who "I" am within my community. That's nothing but good for relationships!

Multi-Modal. By the shear nature of inventories, there is the opportunity to learn about modality at a deeper level for individuals and communities. Additionally, inventories are often taken and scored in a variety of modalities.

Connect to Real Life. Since the "I" in inventories is more or less consistent (I go with me where ever I travel) this information is useful across all content and life activities.

Variations.

Making sure that inventories to be used are accessible to all students is crucial. Consider language and ability challenges and how you will overcome them. Confer with colleagues who have met those challenges well or who deal with specific populations (English Language Learners, Special Education, etc).

Quad Row   B

Description:

Take a piece of paper and divide it down the middle both ways so you have four equal boxes.

In the first box, write: What do you already know about (the topic or subject matter)?

In the second box, write: What do you hope to learn about (the topic or subject matter)?

Prep Time: About 10 minutes for setting up the chart papers for the walkabout version.

Materials: Chart paper and markers for the walkabout version. Handouts found on Magic Resources for the other versions.

In the third box, write: How do you hope to learn about (the topic or subject matter)? – think about learning styles.

And in the last box, write: What do you think you will be able to do after learning about (the topic or subject matter)?

These are then presented to the learners. How they respond is up to you. In small groups or one on one you can do it with a piece of paper and have them draw or write their responses. For small to large groups you can put each question on a piece of chart paper and put them on the wall. Learners can write their responses on a sticky note or directly on the paper. They can also work in small groups and come up with responses together to post for the larger group.

This is obviously an activity designed to introduce a new topic, concept or subject matter. Question 1 helps to establish prior knowledge and can allow you to better understand where all your students are (or are not) in relation to the conversation.

Question 2 and 4 are designed to provide you with insight but to also provide a bit of pre-engagement for the learner. With both questions, there is an invitation to participate and succeed so that learning isn't just expected to happen to the learner.

Question 3 is an invitation for the learner to consider how they might best learn the new information. The question could be expanded to look for activities to consider or to get some additional thoughts about how best to give students access to the content. As the teacher/leader, you would be well served to pay attention to the responses, even if you've done trait inventories and know your students learning style preferences. Remember that learning style preference can vary within the same individual based on the content. General auditory learners may become visual learners specifically in math, for example.

This question can also provide insight into growth in individuals and groups based on an activity or style that is being considered that might not be an actual preference.

Question 4 provides the natural connection to other content and real life, asking the inherent question of "why are we learning this" within an action based model of "then what will you do with it." Like question 1, it's a great way to support learners linking what they already know and do with what they are learning.

Discussion will be important. It is the chance for learners to learn from one another and to see their perspectives validated. Additionally, there is community building that happens in all discussion.

Lastly, it is in the conversation that, in the event important concepts and connections have been overlooked, you can interject them in a natural manner that is less like telling and more like sharing. Dialog can go a long way in establishing the leader as credible as well as part of the community.

Strategies:

Relationship Building. The discussion component of this activity provides ample opportunity for community building and for building relationships within and across the classroom. Be sure to reinforce the rules and guidelines as the discussion begins.

This is another way to also create credibility and safety in you as the learning leader.

Prior Knowledge. Question 1 specifically and question 4 more generally both encourage connection to what is already known.

Connect to Real Life. As discussed above, question 4 provides the opportunity to connect what is being learned to life outside and beyond the classroom. If the learners don't make the leap on their own, you can always prompt it during the discussion.

Movement. Particularly if the questions are individually posted on the walls for students to do a walk-about and answer as individuals or small groups, actual movement is involved.

Variations.

Walk-about. This is the discussed option of writing the individual questions on chart paper and posting them throughout the room. Learners can write on sticky notes and post them to the papers or write directly on the papers. You can also decide if you want to hear from individuals or small groups. This variation works well in partners for inclusive classrooms where students may need to support one another in clearly expressing themselves or moving about the classroom.

1:1. One on one can be between the teacher and one student or between two learners. The handout can be used (or created) that allows the pair to document and discuss their answers.

In a learner pair, it is also useful to have them record their partner's responses on a separate sheet. This encourages listening and clarity.

Rubric Design   B

Description:

Scoring rubrics are pretty common. As a community tool, rubrics can be used to personalize assessment. It is a way to garner individual and group buy in for the assessment as well as for the assignment.

Prep Time: Other than discussion with learners about what a rubric is and how it works, there is no specific prep required.

Materials: Markers, white board or chart paper to note discussion.

Based on the group's understanding of the function and use of the rubric, your role in guiding will vary from in-depth, hands on to aloof and guiding.

First conversation relates to the language of the scale. The goal is to be inclusive, descriptive, and clear. It can include words like excellent to poor or wow to hmmmm or any other appropriate expletives. The scale might be better represented by pictures or emoticons. This initial dialog and decision needs to be something the entire community embraces. It supports the idea of investment from everyone.

As the rubric is crafted, ensure that students remember that they get to decide where they will fall on the assessment scale as they work to complete the project. This entire mechanism supports building to higher order or executive brain functioning. Building a rubric is about creating the assessment and evaluation. (Remember those are the top of the higher order thinking pyramid discussed in Chapter 3.)

There are plenty of rubric examples at Magic Resources that you can provide to your students for samples of what it might look like. The samples provide a variety of language so as to provide more things for students to think about.

Strategies.

Relationship Building. Designing a rubric as a community does nothing but add to relationships. Be sure to utilize the rules and guidelines to manage the process, behavior, and language. This will also increase your trustworthiness and credibility as you provide for a positive experience for all learners.

Predictable Structure. A rubric alone provides for predictability in expectations related to expectations, performance, and assessment. The more experience students have with them, the more solid the predictability.

Multi-Modal. Rubrics can include multi-modal mechanisms of assessment, providing the guidelines for all creative expressions in the assignment; artwork/pictures, lecture, video, audio, etc.

Variations.

Group. The activity discussed is about a community or classroom based rubric and the group development of it. Additionally, a community can vote on an already designed rubric, given multiple choices.

Individually Designed. Similarly, individuals or small groups can be encouraged to design their own rubric based on their project and their intentions. This works really well when individuals or small groups have choices on their expressive projects.

The 10 Rule   D

Description:

Prep Time: None.

Materials: None

The 10 rule is simply about how to set up instruction. Every one's brain can only focus for so long before it needs to shift focus or wander off. Even for adults, 15 minutes of doing the same thing (sitting still and listening, for example) is a long time. As a general rule, it is best to consider doing nothing for more than 10 minutes regardless of the age of the group with whom you are working.

This is quite reasonable when you think about it. Ten minutes of new content is A LOT. It is well worth the time to check for understanding in that short amount of time. I don't follow very many people for more than 10 minutes without having a chance to talk too. It's part of my processing. Talking every 10 minutes isn't required, however. It's just my preferred processing style. There are other ways.

What might it look like? I might introduce a new topic in, let's say, science. I am talking about the difference between an animal cell and a plant cell. As a class, we have previously discussed first an animal cell and then a plant cell. That's the prior knowledge on which I am building. Now I go through and identify what the differences are. Here's a chart that I present:

	Animal Cell	Plant Cell
Cell wall	Absent	Present (formed of cellulose)
Shape	Round (irregular shape)	Rectangular (fixed shape)
Vacuole	One or more small vacuoles (much smaller than plant cells).	One, large central vacuole taking up 90% of cell volume.
Centrioles	Present in all animal cells	Only present in lower

	Animal Cell	Plant Cell
		plant forms.
Chloroplast	Animal cells don't have chloroplasts.	Plant cells have chloroplasts because they make their own food.
Plasma Membrane	Only cell membrane	Cell wall and a cell membrane
Flagella	May be found in some cells	May be found in some cells
Lysosomes	Lysosomes occur in cytoplasm.	Lysosomes usually not evident.
Cilia	Present	It is very rare.

Once I have given them this information, I might divide the room in half and have the left side be the plant cells and the right side be the animal cells. Remember, I've only talked for about 10 minutes. That's enough time to read through the chart. (Yes, they all have a copy of the chart in front of them).

The rules are that the entire cell (all the students on that side of the room) have to raise both hands into the air when I read something that is true about their cell.

I then randomly read from the chart.

I can switch sides of the room to make sure students know both cells or save that for another day. I spend about 10 minutes doing this. Then move on to the next part of the lesson.

In this way I move through content and check for understanding before moving forward. This is particularly useful when working with content that will build on itself as the learning moves forward.

As a trainer, I use these mechanisms a lot, particularly when I am working with skills and want learners to have a chance to experience using the new strategy. This moves the content into the executive functions very effectively.

This example, of course, directly relates to multi-modal presentation.

Yet this complexity isn't required. You can also provide students with questions or have them ask their own. You can have them jot down the 3 most significant things you said, from their perspective.

It isn't about what is done as much as it is about breaking it up into manageable pieces. Remember, it's easier to move a mountain one stone at a time.

Strategies.

Multi-Modal. This example is clearly multi-modal. Finding ways to provide information in multiple modalities becomes easier when we remember the 10 rule. In a 50 minute class, I can introduce 5 different ways of thinking.

Predictable Structure. When learners know that the learning experience will be manageable they are willing to give more and invest at higher levels of their own intellect and endurance.

Variations.

Chunking. This is much the same concept without a dictated structure of 10 minutes. It easily accomplishes the same thing as long as the quantity remains manageable. Material is simply chunked into logical pieces that are then addressed one at a time with a comparative break in the middle. The break is utilized to deepen meaning or check for understanding.

Rotational Instruction | D

Description.

Rotational instruction sets up a blended learning environment that allows for such things as multi-modal presentation, integration of technology, as well as varied accommodations for student ability and disability. It is similar to what has been historically known as "stations."

Prep Time: The amount of time it takes to design the "stations" (lesson plans), gather and set up the materials. There is also the pre-teach for how the rotation works and informs students where they start and how they move.

Materials: Varies.

In the best situation, there are 4 learning environments within the learning environment. The first one is generally large group, introduction of content. If one is integrating the activities presented here, it would be the first 10 minutes of content delivery, done with the class as a whole group.

There are then three other stations. Each one has its own activity, assignment, and/or expectation. Based on the needs within the learning group, I can manipulate the groups to include opportunities for one on one work with those students I know will need it. One station will be a small group project and one will be technology based, provided I have the access to computers or tablets. The third one might be a more advanced opportunity that has more than one option based on what "advanced" means to students.

With rotational instruction, I have the ability to manipulate the content delivery and meet the needs of groups and individuals without over structuring or calling attention. It also provides for natural integration of movement and varied learning style integration.

Small groups can be set up so there are roles within the group (leader, scribe, council, etc.) or can be a more open discussion or project driven assignment (make a poster; read this article and summarize, etc.). You can have a series of small groups, each reading part of a relevant article that they then have to piece together in a large group presentation.

One on one intervention and support can be provided at any station, based on how it is set up and what the student needs. It can also be set up so that students are paired, using each other as the one on one. One student can read to another to increase comprehension. Another student can read to the other to improve fluency. Math buddies can check one another's work and discuss process. The list goes on and on.

Rotational instruction additionally provides for self-management and provides a high level of freedom to the teacher to create a variety of learning opportunities crafted to meet the needs of all the students. It encourages the movement to executive order thinking and allows students to take charge of some of their own learning.

Strategies.

Multi-Modal. Rotational instruction provides for lots of opportunity for the inclusion of multiple modalities all at the same time yet one at a time.

Predictable Structure. As students become familiar with the process and their role, they come to predict how the time will proceed and how they can take control of their own learning while supporting that of their peers.

Real Life Connections. Rotational instruction also provides ample opportunity to integrate the learning into life outside the learning environment by posing questions, problems, and experiences that move the material into a different, more relevant realm. By posing questions like "When you are at the grocery, what might you look at to compare one product to anther besides price?" when content has been exploring compare and contrast.

Self-Check Cards D

Description.

Teaching students to regularly check themselves for understanding is an important self-management skill. The Self-Check Cards are a way to support students in reflecting and communicating their state of understanding.

Prep Time: about 15 minutes initially with students. Time to cut and create the 3 card set for each student.

Materials: 3-card set for each student. 1 green, 1 yellow or orange, and 1 red.

Each student has three cards that sit on the corner of their desk or space. The cards are red, green, and yellow or orange. The object is for the learner to rate their current level of understanding and reflect that in the card that is on top of the pile of the three cards. Green means they are just fine, understanding everything. Yellow/Orange indicates there might be some confusion or they have a question. Red means they are lost or are having trouble making connections.

The training and reinforcement with the learners on how to utilize the cards is integral to its success. Noting body language that you can then reflect and ask the learner whether they have a question is one way to support the process. At that point, you also indicate that the yellow card should be on top.

Another crucial component in the success of this activity is to respond when to the colors shown. When a yellow/orange card is on top, looking to the student and probing for what they need for clarification, "Do you have a question?" or "Is something not making sense?"

As a community, this will also be an exercise in the climate. What is desired is a safe place to ask questions, to not know all the answers, and to sometimes (or more often) not understand. Within the relationships in the group, there might also be a natural tendency to support one another. A student may respond to another student by answering a question. This is a great opportunity since often times how learners talk to each other is more effective than the leader. This has to do with development in content knowledge as much as anything else. As the leader, I know my stuff inside out and upside down. As emerging learners together, the development of the content knowledge has a different perspective that may more readily meet the needs of another learner.

The primary purpose is to provide space and opportunity for learners to recognize their own learning process and when it might be helpful to have additional information. This goes a long way in establishing self-regulation and higher order thinking.

Strategies.

Relationship Building. This activity adds to the relationship between learner and leader as well across learners. It provides space for those who don't potentially process more slowly or differently in a way that is respectful and responsive. Self-check cards can help to bridge gaps in content delivery for students with varying abilities and across cultures. It may also be that the language the leader uses is different from that which a learner (or group of learners) is familiar. The self-check mechanism allows that to be caught early so the active concept can be integrated and built upon.

Multi-Modal. Self-Check Cards allow for self-expression in a non-verbal, visual modality. Additionally, it translates emotions, something that can feel nebulous, into something more concrete. It provides articulation for something for which it is not always easy to find the words.

Predictable Structure. Utilized as part of the routines and habits of the classroom, self-check cards become part of what is predictable within the classroom. It makes not knowing safe and asking questions encouraged. This is exactly what we've discussed in Chapter 6.

Variations.

Mood Check. The self-check cards can also be used to check in with students for moods. It doesn't require anything different in materials, just a different explanation. And it can simply be a change up one day.

Let's say it's the Monday after spring break and I want to be able to gage my learners' overall moods. I can simply say, "Let's take out our Self-Check Cards. I'd like you to quickly do a self-check and let me know how you're doing today. Are you glad to be back and excited to get started with school again? That would probably be a green. Maybe it was hard to get up this morning but you're getting back into the swing of it, albeit slowly. That would probably be a yellow. Then again, it might be that you don't want to be here and wish you didn't have to come back today. That would be a red."

With an established, safe climate and culture the students will provide pretty honest feedback and I get a bit of information that can be helpful in executing my day.

Impromptu. They can also be used more as a tool of intrigue. "Who's ready for a break? Let me see a green card on top of your Self-Check Cards if you're ready right now, yellow if you need a minute or two, and red if you'd rather not have a break."

Overall the self-check can be used to take the pulse of individuals and groups to see what and where they are at any given time. How they are used supports learners as individuals within groups; both of which creates its own dynamics.

Elbow Partners   D

Description.

Elbow Partners is a variation to a common theme. Familiar titles include Think-Pair-Share, Teach-OK, and Learning Buddies.

Pairing learners up into Elbow Partners is the first step. This

Prep Time: 10 minutes to explain and set up with learners.

Materials: None. Can require various materials depending on how they are paired.

can be done randomly or intentionally. As a trainer, it's much more fun to do it intentionally randomly. It prevents people who know each other from staying inside their bubble. This works particularly well when you don't know the learners.

In an extended learning situation, there is more time to intentionally pair learners together. If trait inventories have been completed, they can inform the process. Often times I just use seating to provide me with options. I have them count off by twos, by hippo and chimp, or by 2 letters of the alphabet then have them find their opposite. Depending on the number of learners, you can use a deck of cards and have hearts with diamonds, same number together, etc. It is important that there be a differentiation between the two so that instructions can be coined to match (i.e. who will speak to whom first, etc.). Whatever the mechanism to create the elbow partners, make it clear and something that won't hold up the learning process.

Once each learner knows who their elbow partner is and who they are in the partnership (are you 1 or 2, hippo or chimp, heart or diamond, etc.) it's time for the explanation. It shouldn't take but a few minutes to make the expectations clear.

"Throughout our learning experience there will be time I tell you to find your Elbow Partner. I will also give you instructions like, hippos will talk first or chimps will be the listeners or something similar. To be clear, first I say FIND your elbow partner. Then I give the instructions. Then I will tell you to start. Got it?"

Pretty straightforward, really.

Elbow Partners is one way to apply the 10 Rule. After 10 minutes of content delivery, I can say, "Find your Elbow Partner. Chimps, I want you to tell your partner three things that make an animal cell different from a plant cell. Ready? Go!"

I provide them with about 2 minutes. Then I say, "Hippos, you now need to repeat to your partner the three things they just told you were different between a plant and animal cell. Ready? Go!"

This reinforcement is important. It provides the multi-modal support of hearing and speaking. I would probably repeat the process with the hippos being the lead and the chimps being the repeat. That way there are six pieces of information exchanged.

Elbow Partners can be the same throughout a class time, a day, a week... You can determine when the best time to switch might be.

Strategies.

Relationship Building. Anytime we pair people up, they are in relationship. When they have to work together cooperatively, it is not about whether I like you but whether we can work effectively together. This is a crucial learning in relationship building. That, of course, is in addition to the great opportunity to explore more about who I like and who I work best with, all important components of relationships and understanding how they work for me.

Multi-Modal. Elbow Partners is all about speaking, hearing and saying in a different way. That's all part of multi-modal learning.

Variations.

2-Elbows. There are opportunities when working in groups of three or where two Elbow Partner pairs would do well to work together. This is a way to create small groups, to allow for odd numbered participants (21 people in the room instead of 20 or 22), and learners who need a little extra support.

You can intentionally pair the pairs or create groups of three instead of two. You can also move between having pairs and having small groups made up of two or more pairs. The matches are endless.

Journaling   D

Description:

Maybe this seems obvious, but I've met enough people in learning leadership positions who

Prep Time: None.

Materials: Something for learners to write on and with.

don't use the idea of having learners write things down that I thought it was worth mentioning here.

I define journaling as writing down your thoughts, ideas, feelings, observations, or other insights in the form of words, pictures, renditions, symbols, or other tangible form.

One of the things we know about people is that there are introverts and extroverts (as preferences, not as personality traits!). There's all kinds of information out there about both. Journaling is a useful tool for both, though it tends to be a relished tool for introverts.

That said, everyone should have the opportunity to journal. By providing insightful prompts, journaling can quickly provide space for relationship development, content reinforcement, as well as creativity and design.

I enjoy thinking outside the box, giving people a chance to journal after reading, watching, or hearing potentially emotional content. I always have discussion time afterward to provide room for external processing for those who need it as well.

Yet, not all journaling requires processing time. Nor does all processing time require all leaners to participate. This is where knowing your content and understanding your learners will be a huge asset.

As a professional development trainer and speaker, I often have my participants write things down. Sometimes it's in the form of a formal journaling exercise but most often it's in the form of lists, quick thoughts, or ideas. Often these are related to additional work and used as reference. Sometimes they are more for the individual. Journaling can happen in words, pictures, symbols, or a combination of any or all.

Some examples of journaling I've used:

- Showing pictures of words or people, have them write down a specific number of words that pop into their heads (1, 3, 5)
- Write down a list of everything you see that is red.
- On a self-addressed post-card, write down something you have learned today that you want to apply in the next 6 months. I will mail it to you to remind you.)
- Journal about riding to school in a unique form of transportation (horse, UFO, limo, etc.)
- Explain to your future self how what you learned in this workshop impacted your life.
- Create a picture, without words, that represents your greatest fear about being a teacher.

Journaling also doesn't require table and chairs. There can be poster boards or chart paper to write on scattered throughout the room with a variety of prompts, it can be done laying on the floor, and it's been fun to watch learners find their most comfortable place in a learning environment to stretch out and journal.

I hope this provides some new thoughts for your own experience.

Strategies:

Multi-Modal. Journaling can be done with words, pictures, even sounds and a variety of textures. It is a great way to integrate varied modalities by assigning specific parameters within the assignment. You can have learners use at least three different styles of handwriting, include emoticons, or develop a video or audio for their representation. The possibilities....

Prior Knowledge. Journaling is a great way to help learners make connections to what they already know. This can be done in compare and contrast or questions about how things are related or integrated.

Connect to Real Life. Like prior knowledge, journaling can help learners connect new content to real life application through prompts and free flow.

Variations.

The Unlined Thought. Provide learners with blank, unlined paper. Often times it's amazing what the lack of restriction brings out.

Re-lined Consciousness. Stream of consciousness is another form of journaling that can be fascinating as it relates to new content and how individuals apply it to their own internal processes. By providing lined paper and having the learners first turn the paper 90°, so the lines run top to bottom instead of right to left, have them now write their stream of consciousness. For some people, the influence of the lines can be powerful.

Graphic Organizers   D

Description:

Graphic organizers are a great way to support more visual learners in taking notes and presenting information. The objective is to provide a logical mechanism that allows for note taking and review of the notes taken in a way that informs and supports recall.

Prep Time: Teaching learners to use graphic organizers can take 10 minutes or a couple hours depending on the tool and the learner.

Materials: See the Magic Resources or do an internet search.

There are lots of formal systems out there including Mind Mapping and Venn Diagrams. There are also less formalized mechanisms that are content specific such as sentence and paragraph structures or tools that help students identify the main subject of a paragraph or article and the supporting details.

Regardless of which ones you choose, teaching students how to use the tool is the first crucial step. I find the most effective way to teach it is by doing one together and then providing a practice series, depending on the complexity of the tool.

This allows me to model, guide, watch as they develop, and intervene as needed to avoid having to re-teach (which is what happens when it is taught wrong in the first place). It also gives learners a chance to play with the tool to ascertain if it fits their needs.

Graphic organizers need not limit to words. Pictures can just as easily provide clear information and allows for translation of auditory linguistic into visual pictorial.

Strategies.

Multi-modal. Graphic organizers integrate visual and auditory. The act of writing can also serve as kinesthetic. Teaching learners how to translate what they hear into something they see is an important life-long skill.

Prior Knowledge. Graphic organizers can support linking what is being learned to what is already known, particularly if the connection is visually represented in the organizer. An example might be using a ninety degree angle to explain the concepts of obtuse and acute angles.

Variations.

The variations are endless. See the Magic Resources for more examples.

Giant Board Game   D

Description.

Board games are generally fun. Learning is fun. Putting them together seems natural.

I have created about 50 movement tiles out of fabric, 10 of them in 5 different colors. These allow me to create a myriad of games on the floor of the learning environment for at least 9 different games that I have developed related to content I teach.

Prep Time: The time it takes to make the parts. Set up requires about 10-15 minutes.

Materials: Depending on the variation, you need movement tiles, dice or spinner, objective, question cards, and prizes.

The tiles are set up on the floor in a pattern, designed from a start point to an objective or goal point. I have two additional tiles that are marked as "start" and "finish." I then have cards created specifically to content.

One of the games I play is related to conflict. The cards are designed to provide scenarios that teams have to provide a response for in order to move the number of spaces identified on the card. The format of the response is on the card and takes the form of a song, a skit, or a sculpture. Teams have 10 minutes to create their answer. In each round, teams create simultaneously, each working on a separate card. If the response is correct, they have one team member who serves as the mover who moves through the board to get to the end. The team who gets to the end first wins. I usually give chocolate to the winners (though I have had to be mindful to have alternative choices available too).

I have also set up two simultaneous boards in differing colors that teams run a relay on where the answers all have to connect to each other. This works great for teaching the alphabet in American Sign Language. The team members line up on the tile markers. The first person fingerspells a word starting with the letter 'a'. The next person fingerspells a word starting with the last letter of the previous word. And so on. It's about speed and clarity.

These are just quick examples. There are endless ways to play giant board games where students answer questions in order to move forward. It can be set up in teams or small groups. It also works well in small learning groups individually.

Based on the questions and how the game is set up, you can easily connect new content to prior knowledge as well as real life connections.

Strategies.

Multi-Modal. By nature, learners are being kinesthetic, auditory, and visual in the activity regardless of their role in the process.

Movement. Movement is guaranteed in game playing. How big, how fast, how far, can all be part of the rules of the game and so become more able to be manipulated.

Variations.

Jeopardy. This requires a board divided into squares with $ amounts, cards with relevant answers, and teams.

Concentration. This is a good way to reinforce visuals. I use it most often for symbols, foreign language alphabets, and street signs.

Scavenger Hunt   D

Description.

Prep Time: 0-30 minutes.

Materials: List of objects to be scavenged with rules and parameters. If you are locating objects then you need those and any permissions or arrangements for things to be safe.

Every group I have ever done this with has had a great time and learned a lot. First is the list. I have a disabilities awareness training where I send people out on their lunch break with a list of common objects (paper cup, pencil, and penny) that they have to figure out how to get from strangers without talking. They are also not allowed to show them the list (That rule came as a result of a creative participant), or write anything down. This was then related to common experiences by those who have language challenges and/or can't write in the spoken language.

Another scavenger hunt, I had hidden a large number of erasers in the shapes of pumpkins, bats, candy corn, and black cats (guess which holiday!). There was a time limit and the kids had to find as many as they could of each item. We then counted them, graphed them and discussed greater and less than and compared it to the number of each object I started with (resulting in another search for the left overs). Their reward was they each got to keep an eraser of each shape.

I have also used the ice breaker of a list of statements that then they have to find another person in the room to whom it applies. Can only use each person's name once and you have to ask the question, you can't just hand them the paper. It might say something like "has a tattoo," "was born in a different country," "grew up with more than three siblings," etc.

This is an activity that allows for community building within and across teams. That means it is of particular note that the rules and guidelines be applied while the hunt progresses.

Strategies.

Movement. The scavenger hunt provides a mechanism to increase movement and give people an opportunity for gross motor activity. This is important in brain function too!

Multi-Modal. Most of the modalities and their layers are included in this activity.

Variations.

Safari. By adding a challenge into the acquisition of each object, it easily becomes a safari. Perhaps there has to be a math fact race between two people to determine who gets first pick or, in the case of just one object being available, gets the object.

Logic Scramble. This can be a scavenger hunt of clues that lead to a solution. If the first clue leads to the handicapped stall in the bathroom and the second one to the elevator and the third clue to braille on the ATM machine the solution would be accessibility. This requires some reasoning skills that connect what's been learned to real life and prior knowledge.

Magic Resources

All the resources, research, and other information that you might want access to can be found on a special website created just for this book.

This mechanism has enabled me to reduce the cost of the book and provide you with quality resources, many of which I have created. In this way you can print out full size, usable tools and samples of tools. You can also adapt and manage many of them for your personal use.

There are two ways to get there:

From your smart phone (loads to a mobile site):

To access the website via any browser:

http://with-respect.com/magic-resources/

I hope this serves you well. Your feedback is appreciated:

leah@with-respect.com

About Leah R. Kyaio

My story is real. An inner city kid with a little support who is out to change the world. Never forgetting where I came from, and the fact that there are more still there, I'm reaching out to the world with a message,

"What I do to you, I do to me. What I do to me, I do to you."

I'm out to change the world and invite you to be part of

The 16%.

That's the tipping point, the hundredth monkey. All it takes for us to change the world.

Want to learn more about it? Check it out here:

http://with-respect.com/my16/

Leah has been providing hack services to education, non-profits, government agencies, law enforcement, judicial organizations, and businesses for almost 20 years. Her area of expertise is in relationships. Whether it is cultural competence, conflict negotiation, anti-bullying, organizational culture, or transformational change she focuses on what's working to fix what's not.

What's a hack? Self-defined, it's a tool, strategy, or skill designed to address an issue or problem in the simplest, clearest and most critical way to make success most likely. The strategies and activities found within these pages are an example of how her brain works.

If you are interested in learning more about Leah or her business, With Respect, check out her website at

http://with-respect.com.

Interested in having Leah speak at your event, conference, professional development opportunity or community gathering? Call or email and we will do everything we can to make that happen.

Folks who have experienced Leah say things like,

> "I experienced Leah's diversity and cultural awareness training as part of a very non-diverse group of employees. Her methods were inclusive, non-confrontational, determined, and pragmatic, allowing the group to address uncomfortable topics in a bold but non-threatening manner. Since then, I have discovered that Leah lives what she teaches, setting the example in every venue."

> "Every time I hear you, I learn something. Thanks for saying things that no one else is willing."

> "I love Leah's humor and stories. She's always real and it's always so applicable to I do as a teacher."

> "Leah rocks! You take things that seem muddy and make it easy to understand."

> "Leah's passion is palpable. It gives me hope."

Watch for more of Leah's work coming July 2015.

Made in the USA
San Bernardino, CA
26 February 2015